MY PRISON BREAK

Walk Into Your Freedom, Propel Into Your Purpose

Stacy-Ann "Resurrected" Garvey

MY PRISON BREAK. Copyright © 2020. Resurrected Stacy-Ann Garvey. All Rights Reserved.

Printed in the United States of America.

No portion of this book may be reproduced, stored in a retrieval system, or transmitted in any form or by any means, except for brief quotations in printed reviews, without the prior written permission of DayeLight Publishers or Resurrected Stacy-Ann Garvey.

ISBN: 978-1-953759-11-5

Unless otherwise stated, Scripture quotations marked KJV are from the Holy Bible, King James Version (Authorized Version). First published in 1611. Quoted from the KJV Classic Reference Bible, Copyright 1983, by The Zondervan Corporation.

ENDORSEMENT

Ms. Stacy Garvey takes her readers on a riveting odyssey in this book.

Every recount given in this memoir are like scenes from a dramatic film, as she recalls her "resurrection" from drugs, alcohol, and a promiscuous lifestyle, after an encounter with God while serving a prison sentence—something she detailed as a "blessing in disguise."

Ms. Garvey picturesque narrative of her life's transformation from "prison bud" to minister should inspire hope to the unfortunate and misguided.

This is a must have book in your collection as it is easy to read, and its context relatable.

You will not be disappointed.

Bishop O'mar Wedderburn
Author

To the Holy Spirit:

thank You for living inside of me, for guiding, pushing, and daily renewal; for helping me to understand that I am valuable, loved, and favored.

ACKNOWLEDGMENTS

Sincere gratitude and thanks to my parents, Maureen Hamilton "Mommy," you are my heart; I love you beyond words. You walked with me in the wilderness and stood by me; I am forever grateful.

Hector Garvey, thank you for being a father, so I could gain entry to this world. I love you both very much.

To my extended family, I love you.

To my spiritual father, best friend, and confidante, Leostone Morrison. Thank you for never giving up on me and always trusting me to do the right thing. Thank you for holding my hand in good and bad times and allowing me to make many mistakes. You made me understand that I could tell my story.

Bishop Fabion Steele, "Do not let the devil write and end your story." Thank you for your obedience to a girl you did not even know. I will always love you.

Pastor Sheldon Raymond, a "Daddy" in every sense of the word, whose arms are always open. I love you forever. You are my best friend and the very first pastor to let me know there is a purpose on my life.

Pastor Byron Graham, thank you for opening that door and giving me a word to ponder until I got it.

My Prison Break

Pastor Dean Smith and Prophetess Sarah Smith, I remember when you both said that your ministry is to ensure your flock fulfills all that God has ordained them to be, and when that happens, that is when you know you are fulfilling the mandate. I love you both so much, and my prayer is that God will continue to bless you in extraordinary ways that ears have not heard and eyes have not seen.

Reverend Valentine Rodney, you kept pushing me out of the ordinary and thought of me higher than myself. I love and appreciate you. Blessings always.

Paulette Fowler, thank you for calling me daughter and seeing me as a human being when the circumstances said otherwise. I love you always.

Charlene Williams, thank you for treating me well and taking care of me during the journey.

Hillary Dunkley-Campbell, you are the sweetest, kindest, loyal sister/friend. You believed in this book, even before you knew it was being written.

Reverend Latoya Grant-Clarke, I could not have done this without you. When I forgot that I had a book to write, you kept reminding me; you saw what I could not see in myself. God bless you.

Pastor Chaneika Rhoden-Laing, my sister from another mother. How do I say thanks for your love and support when words seem so inadequate? Thank you for believing in me.

Minister Sandra Daley and Prophetess Jacqui D. Hutchinson, thank you so much for listening to the Holy Spirit and becoming a part of my life. I love you, and I receive your love.

Bishop Devon Laird, Pastor Karell Dawes, Bishop Omar Wedderburn, Bishop Gifton Wallace, Minister Latoya Taylor, Minister Donna Satahoo, Nicole Salmon, Elsa Lawrence, Melissa Fairley, Mahalia Thomas, Lilieth Winter, and Minister Patricia Perry, thank you for your continued love and prayers of coverage, pushing me into purpose and for being my family.

Mr. Ian Blackwood, who believed in my transformation and decided to give me a chance, God bless you; may the Lord expand your borders.

I personally want to thank Rushell McDuffus and Tina Terrelonge who worked tirelessly with me to get this book ready. Love you both.

To my Publisher, Crystal Daye, who believed enough in my vision to carry out this task. The Holy Spirit connected us and gave you the driver's seat to make this book a reality. Thank you for sharing your Holy Spirit wealth of knowledge with me; I am forever grateful.

Finally, thanks to everyone who came into my life for their respective seasons. Without you, all this would not have been possible.

Thank you all.

TABLE OF CONTENTS

Endorsement iii
Acknowledgments v
Introduction 11

PART I
THE DESERTED VALLEY

Chapter 1: Taken to the Valley 15
Chapter 2: In The Valley He Restoreth My Soul 19
Chapter 3: Jesus Has The Final Say 25
Chapter 4: It Is finished 33
Chapter 5: Death is Never Final 39

PART II
THE BONES: DEALING WITH ISSUES

Chapter 6: Issues and the Setbacks 49
Chapter 7: The Coffin That Could Not Close 55
Chapter 8: Abort the Abortion 63

PART III
HEALED AND BE MADE WHOLE

Chapter 9: The Bigger Prison 69
Chapter 10: The Analysis 77

Forgiveness 77

Rejection 82

Anger.. 90

Chapter 11: Uncovering the Scars 93

Part IV
Your Pain is Wealth

Chapter 12: Pain Was Necessary 101

Chapter 13: Enduring the Pain 105

Chapter 14: Integrity in Pain 109

Chapter 15: Painful Worship 115

Conclusion 125

About the Author 129

INTRODUCTION

We live in a society that can be very unforgiving; if past mistakes or issues have marred your character, you become afraid to face or even talk about them. Most of these issues have caused hearts and minds to become trapped and blocked, ultimately resulting in one's spirit not being in tune with their soul and body.

My Prison Break will expose issues and topics that persons are afraid to speak of or deal with. It will shed light on the mess that many have buried and seem to have forgotten, but ultimately it still controls them. These issues have caused many to struggle with mental health issues, even as Christians, and ultimately become imprisoned by them.

This book was birthed out of a prison experience, which caused the real prison to be known and acknowledged. It will allow readers to understand that a situation is never as simple as it may seem, or we think it is. This book is expected to change lives, bring forth deliverance to captives and break limitations. It will empower minds and allow individuals to see the real value within themselves and realise their true selves and God-given potential. It highlights the potential within all, which is unstoppable.

I did not write My Prison Break for sympathy or because it was a good story to tell. I wanted to evangelise the true meaning of God's Word in John 3:16: *"For God so love the world that He gave his only begotten Son that whosoever believes in him should not perish but have everlasting life."* I want persons to know how reckless the love of God really is and that we do have not to pretend in order to receive His love. It highlights that even though my experiences were not the best, they were worth it. This book lets persons know that no matter how dirty, messy, or unattractive some things appear, there is something good on the inside, ultimately bringing transformation and hope.

Giving up is never an option. Being bound is never someone's final portion, except for the devil. We who are created in God's image and likeness have a rich heritage that was provided for us by God, and the circumstances of life should never have the power to keep us bound whereby we are not able to inherit all God has destined for us in His Word. It is written in Revelation 12:11: *"And they overcame him by the blood of the Lamb and word of their testimony; and they loved not their lives unto death."*

I believe God is using this medium to teach us who we truly are and take us to our next level. This is to show us that where we are, no matter how far gone, we can be redeemed, and we can be set free. Our lives can impact those we come across once we display the right attitude, and even those cast aside by society and man can be redeemed.

This book exposes the lies of the enemy "anti-Christ" and promotes the Word, which is God's truth. We were all created to reflect God; this book will bring mind renewal: getting our minds and hearts to a place where we break free from the shackles of captivity and limitations. We will begin to live the life that speaks to resurrection power and transformation through Jesus Christ.

PART I
THE DESERTED VALLEY

CHAPTER 1
TAKEN TO THE VALLEY

Have you ever seen a bone that had been chewed and thrown out? A bone with every substance eaten off; the fluid sucked out, and every ounce of meat taken off? Have you ever stopped and noticed a dry bone? Well, that was me when I arrived at the Fort Augusta Adult Correctional Centre, a nice name for "Prison." This is where I ended up after twenty-eight years of my life. I went to school and worked for almost eight years with many achievements, just to end up in prison.

I arrived in the deserted valley on March 3, 2010, when I was remanded in custody after a court appearance at the Half Way Tree Criminal Court. I was so clouded, sick, confused, scared, hurt, and even angry. How I felt did not help me to get out of the valley I was in. Funny enough, I could not blame anyone but myself. I did not know what to think, what to do, what to say, even how to say what I wanted to say. All I could do was just say, "Mommy, help me."

I was four months pregnant with a baby I did not want and tried aborting, but the baby would not leave me. When I found out I was with child for the eighth or ninth time, I had no idea what I was going to do. I had a case in court, and I was not in a steady relationship. The man I was seeing was married with two children. In my mind, dating this person was just for fun and an antidote for the pain I was experiencing. I was a loose cannon, a time bomb, no direction, no sense of worth, and no common sense. There was nothing logical about my thinking. All I was interested in was the drug taken to help me sleep; smoking, drugs, and alcohol made me numb and shut out the world. I was already in the prison of depression, without even being conscious of what depression was.

I remember telling the young man that I did not want the child; I had no regrets. I had no regrets because I had gotten so used to abortions; this was probably my seventh or eighth, so it was nothing new. The father was on his own, had no impact on me and that is what being numb to life can do to someone. You are so numb that you do not even care about the life you are blessed with. I remember doing what was needed to get rid of this child, but he just would not leave. I heard the words, "You cannot kill what God has anointed."

I had another son who was three years old, and I was so caught up in my sorrows and depressing life that I could not take care of myself emotionally. How was I to take care of my son who, I must say, was the love of my life and one of the few who stood up for me. As a baby, you could not say a bad word about me within his hearing or he would certainly have an answer or take up a stone ready to fight. Due to my case and everything that was happening with me, I missed out on so much time with him.

I turned into a dry bone and was thrown into the valley of dry bones. In the valley, nothing matters anymore. Status did not matter: where I was from or where I had been; nothing matters. The fact is, we all end up in the valley for one reason or another, and we all look the same. In the valley, it did not matter who you knew; all that mattered was who knew you. Out of all the people I knew, only my mother and a few family members knew me: no joke. In the valley, no one outside of the valley has time to consider you or care for you, except, as I said, if they knew you. If they remember your kindness, compassion, and genuinely loved you, then, in the midst of your valley, they will remember you.

I had planned the final suicide attempt in prison. I wrote the letters to my mother and the judge, even to some people I knew. But there is a man called Jesus, and even sometimes when we do not remember Him, He remembers us. Jeremiah 1:5 says, *"Before I formed thee in the belly, I knew thee and before thou comest forth out of the womb I sanctified thee, and ordained thee a prophet unto the nations."*

I never understood that the Word of God cannot lie; neither can it be null and void; what God has spoken must come to pass. Even if we live our lives separated from God due to sin, His Word said He already knew us. Since He knows us and how our future and stories are to be written, our destiny must be according to how God has spoken and predestined it. Nothing can stop God's ordinance, nothing: not even prison. This was not my first suicide attempt. Prior to getting remanded in custody, I attempted suicide while I was also pregnant.

I forgot about Jesus when my life got crowded by a man, bling, and pleasures. I laid God aside and moved on with the world. I had status, and I unconsciously thought I could do without God. After all, I had seen so many things happen, and, in my eyes, money was the only solution for everything. In my eyes, once you had money, you could solve any problem. When I got in trouble with the law for the first time in October 2008, I spoke to a lawyer, and he let me know what money could do for me. He did not explain that money would not take me away from the valley or prevent me from reaching the valley, if God was going to allow the valley to teach me a lesson so I know He is God. The valley was to show that He is to be praised, to teach me the lesson that He created the heavens and the earth, and no one has the power to breathe life, except Him. I wonder if, while reading this, your understanding of who God is and His power will be clearer. God is a jealous God.

My Prison Break

I tried suicide to get rid of my troubles and escape my valley, but God was not having it. He was not about to let me give up when He was not finished with me. He had work for me to do even when I was in prison. God wanted me to understand where I was, who I was, what my purpose was and to understand that He knew me before I was born and I was a chosen vessel; very special to Him.

The plan was set: I was going to hang myself in the dorm when everyone was out, either at work or relaxing outside. I had the sheet and had placed the written letters somewhere they could be easily found. I took the sheet and was walking to the back of the dorm when the lunch bell rang; I could not do it again. I became so upset and angry that I did not even take lunch. I did not want to eat. There was a Christian lady there who I got upset with and gave the letters to. After reading them, she started crying out to Jesus on my behalf. She took a book of encouragement for me to read, and, honestly, it did not make a difference because I still wanted to die.

CHAPTER 2
IN THE VALLEY HE RESTORETH MY SOUL

I struggled with myself for days. I could not get any sleeping pills or cannabis to help me sleep because everyone was aware that I was pregnant. I was not sleeping. I had the same mindset every day: I wanted to go home, but then the reality always hit me that this is home for now.

I started working at age eighteen because I wanted my independence. I did not grow up with much, but I was always satisfied. I did not realise my family was poor. We grew up being satisfied with what we had. We ate whatever was available; most times, we drank water. We were happy children. We did not realise there was more to life than bread and butter mornings. My grandmother, Linneth Euphena Garvey, God rest her soul, was one of the kindest women I ever met. She kept the family together and taught us how to be content with whatever stage we are at. She was a praying woman who taught us from an early age that prayer is key. There was a lesson of love that she taught in her own way but not in the way that could have rescued me from the jaws of rejection that took up residence in my life pretty early, and later caused mayhem.

There was a time when I considered myself the black sheep of the family. I behaved, spoke, and acted differently. When everyone was quiet, I was loud. When everyone had no opinion, I had plenty. When everyone accepted things as they are, I always felt they could be different. So, I was known as the mouthpiece of the family, even at a young age. I always knew there was more to life but never confirmed it until I was eighteen and began working. I began to see life in a different light. I saw where I could achieve so much because I believed I could, so I developed an independent go-getter mentality that was fearless. This led me to start doing things early. I realised that if I believed in myself, the sky was not my limit because I could soar far beyond the sky. Due to this mentality, I did not allow anything to keep me broken because I learned the art of covering my issues with my go-getter mentality. So, the issues began blocking my soul in such a way that my spirit man had difficulties getting through to Stacy-Ann Garvey.

When I began working and I got my first salary, it was the first time I ever received so much money in my eighteen years of existence. I thought about what to do with it. It was the first time in my life I felt rich. I did not know that you could be "penny wise but pound foolish." I began using my salary to spend on friends and family as I had nothing else to do with it. My grandmother would have been so proud, and I believed kindness was also a weakness for me. I believed that if I were kind enough to people, then maybe they would love me for me. I did not understand that when people see your kindness, they see it as a doorway to your weakness. Looking back, trying to buy love is what happened because I believed that money could buy love. I did not understand that the love I so desperately needed was there waiting for me all along. Jesus Christ demonstrated love when He sacrificed Himself on that cross so we could all have life.

I laid there on that prison bunk bed, trying to wonder if anyone really loved me. It took hours to go through the checklist, which led to probably only about three persons.

I remember the first relationship I had. I was so in love because the young man said he loved me. That was something I desperately needed to hear and feel, and I would do anything to keep that love. I was in church following in my grandmother's footsteps and reading the Bible that says fornication is a sin. I was willing to let my body be a sacrifice to keep the love I so desperately needed. One day that "love" got tired of me and decided he did not want me anymore. He moved on to greener pastures. The fact is, this experience allowed depression to first enter my life. I did what I knew how to do: cover it up with my go-getter mentality. I went "hard" because I had to surpass expectations, limitations, and barriers. I told myself I would achieve so much, and in achieving, I would look so good that no one would ever be able to deny, object or break who I am or leave me ever again I would do so well in life that everyone just had to fall in love with me I would have so much money that I could buy anyone's love by buying them anything they wanted. The money I had would give me popularity, fame, and respect. Rejection lied so well to me, and I believed it all.

The job I had was the doorway to this aspiration, but depression sat on the lines listening to the sounds I echoed and saw the doorway to walk through. Evil presented itself, and I fell for it. That was exactly where my mind was. I was never forced, never pushed; getting involved in activities that led me to the prison gates was my own free will.

I was never exposed to criminality as a child. I remember once witnessing the death of my stepfather while my mother was running her business. I did not know certain terms; I cannot remember hearing the term "fraud." I knew if people carried drugs abroad, committed murder, or even steal and get caught, they would go to jail. That was as far as I was knowledgeable about the law. I saw all of this on television.

At the company where I worked, opportunities started presenting itself to make extra money. The only thing I was conscious of was the fact that if caught, I would probably be fired. I was numb to objective thinking, logical thinking, or even being sensible. The go-getter mentality had overpowered good sense and integrity. I had a goal, and that was all I was interested in. Thinking straight was irrelevant; it was not even on the peripheral. I got involved in a whirlwind that messed me up, got mixed up, tarnished, assassinated my character, and turned my life upside down. The result of what I was involved in landed me behind the walls of the Fort Augusta Adult Correctional. This happened all because death had rejected me.

One day, while lying on my prison bed, I began thinking, wondering: when did I lose myself and what really caused me to get there? What caused my demise? What caused me to become who I was? Why was I so lost? What caused me to end up lying on a prison bunk bed? For days all I could think about was nothing but my failures. I kept wondering why such a failure presented itself in a life like mine. In my mind, I tried considering how to bargain with the devil to see if he could free me from where I was so I could return to the pills, alcohol, and fun. I wanted to return to the road, but even the devil had given up on me.

A couple of days later, I was in my dorm when I remembered there was an Evangelist lady in the prison name Norma who I thought could offer encouragement to lift my spirit. After all, I remembered that a little gospel could lift depression. So, I wrote a letter asking her to help me pray that I would be offered bail and get to go home. When she read the letter, she came to the dorm and asked me to come and talk to her in the lunchroom, which I did. The lady looked me dead in the eyes and asked, "When you kill yourself, what will be your answer to God about that prophet and preacher boy you are carrying inside your belly?" I froze. I did not have an answer. She asked, "What if you had been successful in killing the prophet you are carrying inside your belly?" I had no words at that moment. I was astonished to know that God still had plans for me and had me on His mind, to consider even lowly me. That day, Norma encouraged me in a way that I had not been encouraged for years. I decided I needed to get more of what she was saying by going to church in the prison because I was now desperate and just needed answers.

CHAPTER 3
JESUS HAS THE FINAL SAY

The first Saturday I went to church in prison, a Minister told us, "There is still hope." He said, "It does not matter where you have been; there is still hope." For some strange reason, I believed the word, and it caused me to want more. I was told that other services would be held over the weekend, so I decided to visit again on Sunday.

The first Sunday in prison, Minister Fabian Steele, who is now Bishop Fabian Steele, and some brethren from the church called House of God, came to minister. I can recall, as I sat in the prison sanctuary that Sunday, the singing and worship made me feel like something was breaking, but I could not tell what. When the man of God began to minister, he read a Scripture and released a Rhema word, "**Do not allow the devil to end your story.**" To date, even while writing this book, I cannot explain that Kairos moment to anyone. The word supernaturally connected with my mind and changed my heart from a place of wanting to die to being ready to live again. The word gave me freedom mentally, even while I was physically locked up and imprisoned. The word echoed transformation, and I moved from deadness to resurrection.

Tears came, but it was not tears of depression and sadness anymore; it was tears saying thanks to God for loving someone like me. At that moment, I wanted to change because I heard a word that echoed the love of Jesus Christ, and it gave life and an encounter with the Holy Spirit that shifted my entire life.

After church, I went to my dorm, sat on the bunk bed, and wrote a prayer to God:

"*Dear God,*

This prayer is about my journey at Fort Augusta. I thought the times when I am hurt, depressed, or in pain and the worries I have would never end. But, more importantly, letting go and letting God. Lord, I came here on the 3rd of March, and I still have not been back to court, and it is now the 11th of March 2010. Believe me, it has not been easy. I have cried, still cry, and I am trying to be strong and hold on to You, God. I think of what life was like and how good I was to people and to see the very few I can now count on. My mother is the only one who is doing everything she can to help me and my unborn child. God, please continue to bless her immeasurably and keep her.

As of today, I am just going to allow You to have Your way in my life. I pray that You become the head of my life. I pray that through Your Holy Spirit, You allow me to first seek You and for You to control me and everything in my life. I pray that You forgive me of my sins and shortcomings. Lord, forgive my foolish thoughts and sinful mind. Lord Jesus, help me that when in doubt, I will be able to say, "Jesus, help me to have a mind of faithfulness to You."

Father God, allow me to understand that You created the earth and us, and You know all about us, and You know especially all about ME: what I am, where I would be today, and You hold my tomorrow. God, You are still the Author and Finisher of my life. No devil in hell, even though I used to trust him, can change that. Into Your hands, Lord, I commit my spirit, mind, body, and soul. Lord, forgive me of my past, and I repent of my sins. Please help me to walk in newness; grant me happiness where there is depression: Grant joy, Lord Jesus. I commit my past hurts and failures to You. They are not worthy of being compared with my future success, prosperity, deliverance, endurance, happiness, and peace of mind. Thank You, Lord Jesus. At this moment, help me to have a better attitude about who I am and where I am. Lord, have Thine own way; continue to have the wheel in my life, in Jesus's name. Amen. And, God, please keep me in prison until You have totally transformed my life, and I am ready for society again."

I again received Jesus Christ from behind prison walls. In other words, I received Jesus in the deserted valley of dry bones. I realised I still had a purpose to witness to the other dry bones present in the valley. I was still on remand, not receiving a sentence, but I saw myself testifying about the goodness of God Almighty, even in my situation. I knew I was being sabotaged with my court case because I was not being taken to court; neither was the case mentioned. The lawyer, who charged me JA$1.9 million, walked away from the case and left me without a leg to stand on. There was so much to keep this dry bone dry, but the Lord sent His servant to minister to me in the valley, and I listened. From then, I started on the road with Jesus.

Hope is what I now have in Christ Jesus, which carried me through my time every day. I became aware of my reality and decided to take it one step at a time. It was like being on drugs; I was actually on drugs. It was slowly beginning to leave my system. I became a free woman while I was still behind bars, and that was one of the best feelings I ever had in years.

After totally submitting to God and receiving salvation, the enemy was still trying to imprison my mind in the days to come. So many thoughts plagued my mind; the past would not leave me alone, and memories just kept coming. I began thinking about how I had so many persons saying things about me, so many pronouncing their own future for me, and enemies predicting my life and what would happen to me. Some people said in the past, "Prison would not miss you." It hurt so bad.

People threw my stupidity in my face; people used me and then laughed. My failures were staring me right in the face, and the hurt just kept coming.

I remember getting a text message from an ex-lover's baby mother, stating that the wrong I was committing and supporting her man allowed her to be comfortable, living in luxury. They toasted to my stupidity with champagne and then laughed. All I could do was look at my life and feel embarrassed. I remember when the text came to my phone; I was driving and had to stop. I only regret that I did not get to tell her she was right, and thank you. The truth is, she was right. I was at a point in my life where I cared about nothing, not even the money. It did not matter who I gave it to or what was done with it; I did not care. I was on a path of destruction with no sanity whatsoever. There was no logic in my thinking, none.

I began dating someone who was like a drug. This person filled the voids I thought I had. This person exposed me to outrageous living: partying, excessive drinking, and what many would call "fun." I saw this person as protection, someone who would have my back. When I met him, the package was neatly presented to me. I had no time to think about their personal life or how I would fit into their life. It felt like I had someone in my corner who listened and who always had my back and best interests at heart. This person seemed so interested in every area of my life, especially the area of my wrongs. There was an adrenaline rush whenever I was around him, which was all that mattered. The other women he was with, those who sought him and who he had, did not matter. Being around him 24/7 made it seem as if I was the only woman who existed in his life. What put the icing on the cake was that he seemingly did everything I wanted, and always listened to me: game well played.

Looking back, I was never in love him. I was in love with what he came with. That was the drug I needed. He was not a physical drug but the mental drug I so desperately needed; the injection I thought was making me live and be better, but I was dead and decomposing around him every day. This man had nothing to offer me; all he did was take and decrease every ounce of sanity that I had left. He had a money agenda. He slept with so many different women and transferred so many spirits to me that it was the grace of God that kept me. The situation was super toxic, and I just existed in it for absolutely no reason. I believe I was there out of guilt because I knew I did not love him, but he had been protecting me with motives, of course.

My life became loose and out of control, and I did not know how to stop it. I met this person at a time when I decided to be rebellious and just do what I wanted as life had hurt me too many times. I was involved in criminal activities and making money, taking drugs, and partying out of control, and he was just the fuel that blazed the fire even more. I was never interested in the life he already had with his child's mother, as it was never in my face. I just cared about the fun and what it was doing for me. I was a very broken woman who had just exploded and did not care anymore. I had gotten in trouble with the law and was just totally far gone from reality.

We partied hard, and the sexual immorality was at another level. This person would have sex with multiple women and then me on the same night or day. I think he was obsessed with me because, no matter what, he was always where I was and behaved hungry for more of me. He behaved as a protector who would fight for me and shield me, but there was so much out-of-control behaviour. I remember partying so hard: drunk, loaded with drugs, and waking up to another woman in our hotel bed and not remembering anything that happened the night before. There were so many demons that had been transferred to me, and they were all destroying my soul. I was with him for a reason I may never be able to fully explain, and he was with me for what I had to offer.

When I got that text from the young lady, all it did was wake me up from the fallacy I was in. I considered how I could get out, but that is all I could do: consider. No answer came. I saw myself being destroyed before my very eyes, and I could not do anything about it. It felt like I had a knife stabbing myself in the heart. I had no control and could not stop. That day, I wondered what happened to me. How did I end up here? I wondered if I could ever be myself again. But that is all I did: wonder and continued on to take some drugs that would cause me to feel high above what was said and drink alcohol to medicate the pain I had felt, thereby falling in the arms of my second child's father. Those arms dried my physical tears at that time; that is all he could do. He had no idea of the mess that he was holding in his hands. Rejection had navigated the decisions I made and was in control of my existence. I was so powerless that I could not even see it or even acknowledge it. The funny thing is, what I was I also attracted because, sure enough, this man, who seemed like a rescuer, was also damaged.

My story has many chapters, and, at that point, without Christ, the chapters were just blank: no meaning, nothing substantial was written. I realised that even though I had a story and had the material to make the story, I was not in control of the pen writing my story. That day, I realised that I allowed the opinion of someone who was shining a light on my stupidity to add to my story. That was illegal and not according to the will of God. I allowed an opinion and the pain of failure to dictate the direction my life had taken. I allowed everything I had gone through to navigate my journey; a journey that I was given the authority to be in charge of: it was MY story. But all I was going through had taken it from me. It was not fair, it was injustice, and it was like being raped and molested simultaneously and being told to shut up, as though I was not worthy of speaking.

So, coming to that realisation, I closed my eyes, and I repented. I repented for not being thankful for the life God had given me; repented for not walking the journey I was given to walk; repented for not being me; repented for living like an illegal alien. I said, *"Lord, I am ready to start writing my own story. Give me the tools needed to sharpen my pencil. Lord, as of today, I take back my authority and, Lord, my life is in Your hands. I am ready to write."*

After hearing Minister Fabian speak and preaching into my spirit as he spoke, I decided that I owned every word uttered. I decided that there was more to my story. Irrespective of what most persons were saying was true or not, it was not the truth in its entirety.

I learned that God's delay is not His denial. I had been praying to go to court, to get bail, and leave the prison before giving birth to my baby. I received five court dates from a lawyer I had, but he did nothing to help because he was not being paid. My mother tried, but nothing worked; the only court date I had was in September, and my baby was due in August.

It was a hard situation to be in. I wished I could be at my mother's home or anywhere but the prison: somewhere to be comfortable, to have the baby in a more sensitive place; a place where sodomy and so many evil spirits were not evident. I wanted to be anywhere I could be more comfortable after the birth of my child.

After I found out I was still pregnant, I did not reach out to his father. For one, it would have been uncomfortable; he had a family, and I did not want to bring my mess into his life. I wanted to leave it where it was. So, I decided to start navigating through the season and trust God: it was now recovery mode.

CHAPTER 4
IT IS FINISHED

I met my second son's father ten months prior to being incarcerated. When I met him, I was not looking for a relationship and did not think he was either. He was just there, and I needed someone to be there. I had no issues with him; he did not seem to have an agenda, and he did not require a lot from me financially. I eventually had to expose my truth so he knew where I was, thereby protecting him from my baggage but little did I know that I also needed protection from his baggage. There was no gain or loss; it was just a situation that existed that was in alignment with a chapter in my story.

When I got pregnant, I told him I wanted to abort the baby because I was not in a position to mother a child. He was not in a position to accept the situation either. So, we both agreed that abortion was the best solution for our situation. I did what I did to get rid of the baby I thought I did not want, and what was done had no bearing on what God had already done. So, I knew the situation at hand would cause turmoil, so I left it and had no more contact at that time.

One of the things the enemy did while in that space, when I was detached from my true self, was to make money seem like the solution. He made me blind and unconscious to God. I believed that once I had money, I could do what I wanted, and that was the true meaning of life. The Bible says, "For the love of money is the root of all evil." (1 Timothy 6:10a). The Lord allowed me to have access to money; He could have blocked it, could have stopped, or stepped in the midst of what I was doing, but He allowed it. Persons think that once you have money, you have it all together; however, that is a lie from the pit of hell. I did so many things to myself once I had money but had no real and genuine love.

I did so many things to myself, trying to find love and peace. I remember having my first son, and the relationship was not working out with his father. I recalled that I had entered the second relationship damaged and tried to make him fix what was wrong from my first relationship where that man had left me, but the second was never the solution to what I was going through. I entered the relationship with him covering up my hurt from previous relationships; he seemed to be the solution. I loved him and what it brought quickly became obsessive and possessive.

This second relationship was toxic. For six years, we continuously argued as our issues started clashing. He wanted to live his life, and I had my version of how he should be living. I wanted to settle and get married while he was still living the life and wanting more than I could give. I remember at a point in the relationship, I would go crazy if I could not find him. When our issues became too much for me, that is when I began to thrive on sleeping pills. Whenever I had issues with him, I just wanted to sleep. That is how I became dependent on sleeping pills and anti-depressants. That was not helping, so I turned to partying and going out, spending excess money even on friends because I thought that was something I had to do to keep people around. I tried to buy my son's father's love. I would buy him really nice and expensive gifts, cook him really great dinners, but nothing worked.

When the relationship did not work, and rejection came in pulling bitterness with it, everything just became too much to handle. I needed a distraction, and that came in the form of tattoos and piercings. I saw those things as drawing attention to myself, which would make me popular and the life of any party. I knew it would draw unusual attention to me. I became obsessed with body art and piercings. I currently have fifteen tattoos and eight different body piercings. I wanted to always stand out; I wanted to always have attention. With all of this, God was still not through with me.

Tattoos and piercings were open doors for the enemy. This is something I learned while in prison watching a Bible Study session on a television one Sunday morning. After watching that program, I had to remove the tongue ring and navel ring because of the strength of the conviction I had. I repented of my sins and thought of Romans 8, reminding me that there is now no condemnation to them which are in Christ Jesus. The old man has been put away, and behold, a new woman of God emerged.

I was a mess without the Holy Spirit to teach me how to be in a relationship, so the truth is, no relationship could ever work, and as I continued, I was only getting worse. The last relationship saw me living the life of an adulterous woman, and that was a curse. I had to make a change, and when the Lord began opening my eyes to who I truly was, I began to receive the transformation; I was still pregnant with my son and incarcerated.

Just because you may be in prison, as I was, does not mean you have to imprison your mind against righteousness or get so caught up in your prison situation that you forget God and who God is and what He can do. Remember Joseph: God allowed him to be taken to prison right there in the midst of his valley. Joseph became great in Egypt. My brother, dare to be a Joseph; my sister, dare to be the female Joseph. I realised that the dead weight had to be shed; the old man had to go, and it did not matter where I was for the shedding to occur. What mattered was that I heard the Word and responded. God began to do a work in me because I heard His Word and accepted.

We can have the mind of Christ. That is the truth. While imprisoned, I learned that God can save and use anyone, even a prisoner. God is able to use anyone or anything for His glory. It does not matter where you have been; He just wants to get you where you should be going.

*"Let this mind be in you, which was also in Jesus Christ." (*Philippians 2:5 – NKJV).

A renewed mind is a mind that operates based on the Word of God; a mind that is not disturbed by the present circumstances, but is focused merely on what the Word of God says. When you have a renewed mind, you do not operate based on self, flesh, or even what you think; you operate on what God says. A renewed mind understands totally that Jesus Christ has the final say. Our lives started with Christ, so it must end with Him. A renewed mind is constantly focused on God's Word, not opinions or situations. We as human beings must understand that we were created to conform; that is, if we are around something long enough, we conform to it.

One of the first things God does for us as children, for us to be saved, is to take us through the process of consecration, so we are identifiable to Him as He is holy. Consecration means pulling away from the old man and clinging to God, who is holy. Clinging is pulling nearer to God. Consecration has two main objectives: transformation (where change takes place) and empowerment (this is as a result of being transformed). You can never truly experience the presence of God and remain the same, not even in prison.

There is no Scripture that shows an encounter with Jesus, and that person remains the same. The primary sign that exhibits an encounter with God is change, and this begins in the mind. This is the change that represents the transformation. During transformation, you will learn discipline and obedience to God; you grow in God.

Transformation requires your will; the stage where you say, "Lord, not my will but Yours." Transformation requires exposure. So, you expose what is in you and let God fill you. You will have deliverance, submission, and honesty.

Empowerment comes as a result of transformation. God did not change you to merely change you. For Him to use you, He must change you to fill you with His presence. Once He changes you, you will have beauty and responsibility. Romans 12:2a says, *"And be not conformed to this world: but be ye transformed by the renewing of your mind…"* It is important for us to understand that transformation takes place before empowerment. God will never give anyone responsibility before they are transformed. We must understand that God knows us on an individual level. He knows my failures and the demons that I was facing. God had to separate me from society, so the drugs and alcohol could not hold me captive, neither could the money corrupt me. He took me through that consecration process.

When you are going through consecration, God deals with your image. In Genesis 1, God gave Adam His image, so Adam was created to reflect God. It is only through the presence of God, which comes through consecration, that we will see our true image. I was created to reflect God, but for years, I was not reflecting my true image. The truth of life is that people would allow sin to conform us. I adapted to everything around me and corrupted my nature. God had to lock me away until I was broken enough to hear and surrender to Him so He could begin the consecration process in my life. Thereby, He truly transformed me into His image and likeness. Upon being transformed, I began to see everything that was wrong with me and started praying for God to make the changes. Right there, behind the bars of the Fort August Adult Correctional Centre, I was consecrated and transformed.

The devil wants you to give up while walking through your transformation; he wants you to throw in the towel or entice you with innumerable evil solutions as a way out of your valley. Do not fall for it. All the enemy is doing is sinking you deeper; find Jesus and hold on to Him. He is the ONLY way, truth, and life.

I remember about two months had elapsed, and I was not being taken to court, and persons inside the prison would approach me and tell stories. I was told that persons were working "science" against me, which I did not dispute based on my case's nature and the people against me; it was quite possible. I was offered solutions to my case, but these solutions came at a price. A man told me that if I had spoken to him as I got into trouble, I would have been out of prison a long time ago, and the list goes on. I live to tell you that there is only ONE God, and nothing is more powerful than Him. If you put your trust in anything or anyone other than the almighty God, you are bound for failure. Trust Jesus Christ and Him alone. I did not need a quick solution; I was glad for my mess because I learned that God can take my messed up situation and turn it into a message. I felt like I was enrolled in a college, understanding life and God all over again. I was walking into my destiny as a minister of the Word of God. In my prison experience, I received the gift of the Spirit, anointing, a love letter from Christ, intimacy, and life.

In order for transformation and empowerment to take place, we must learn that God will allow us to go through some prison situations. He will cause us to be caught between a rock and a hard place, to bring us to a place of total surrender so He can have His way in our lives.

CHAPTER 5
DEATH IS NEVER FINAL

Minister Fabian came on the final Sunday in May 2010, and preached about my situation; it was called "Lazarus." I was dead for years, but Jesus never forgot about me because God was not through with me. My life was filled with so many problems, pain, hurt, depression, addiction, and stress. I did not realise what really mattered and what should not. I lived for the moment, did anything just to get me a high on life, whether it was shopping, partying, or just simply having lots of fun. I made stupid mistakes, allowed people to use me, take advantage and fool me for money because I was blinded by desire or, should I say, infatuation. When I really needed someone, they did not need me. I was a victim of serious rejection.

I tried everything; I lived on pills, it was all I wanted, all I cared for, and when I could not afford the pills, I tried something else. I smoked marijuana (weed) just to feel good and sleep, blocking out my real life. Flesh and blood never mattered at the time; there was nothing like my pills. I did not remember God. I used to go to a spiritualist who brought me to a fire and threw rum when I felt religious or if I needed a solution to a problem. I never realised I was wasting precious time and money. At the time, it felt as if the church was not doing anything for me,` so whatever could help me and make me feel alive, that is what I wanted. After I got into trouble and ended up in the valley of dry bones, everything changed. Loyalty was nowhere to be found; everything that was bad and terrible was happening. I could not look up or feel better; I could not see beyond my problems for deliverance. I did not know what to do. I was on the verge of losing my soul because I had lost everything. It was a "Lazarus" situation; God came and took me from the grave.

When I was in my teens and attending Yallahs Baptist Church, I had my first mentor and a spiritual leader, Orville Vassell. He once told me he had a dream about me. In the dream I was in a coffin; dead, but the coffin could not close. In 2008 when I was first arrested, and I was at the Duhaney Park lock up, a lady also told me she had a similar dream: I was in the coffin that could not close. So, it had been years that the devil has placed me in a coffin, but King Jesus said, "It cannot be closed because I am coming for you, Stacy-Ann." I was past the decomposing, maggots, dirty, nasty, and bloody state; only bones remained. It was then, at that appointed time, God chose to send forth His Son, Jesus Christ, to call me forth. All Jesus had to do was give a sound Word, and He did.

I was imprisoned mentally with what seemed like no hope when I arrived at the prison. My mind kept thinking about the persons I thought would be loyal and have my back by helping my mother so she could help me but chose not to. I was like an outcast who had to end up in prison; my tears were so dry. When persons around me spoke to me about my situation, all I did was look and listen. It hit me that I was in a dry situation. It was a dry situation that could only be called a Lazarus story. But there is something about that man called Jesus. If you have read Lazarus' story, you will better understand what I am about to say to you about the magnificence of who Jesus Christ is.

The Lord said my situation would not end in death and dryness because He knows, and He is the one who breathes life. Understand that as you are reading this, the way Mary sent for Jesus to help Lazarus is similar to my mother crying to Jesus to help me. It seemed as if He was not listening, but He is an on-time God.

It is important for many of us to understand that unless a situation has a stench, there is no reason for a miracle. Some of us were designed to operate at ground level. Some of us were designed to operate a little above the ceiling and some in mid-air. But there are others who God designed and called eagles. Eagles are fearless, tenacious, and high flying. They never eat dead meat and possess vitality while they nurture their younger ones. There is something special about an eagle they have large eyes, hooked beaks for ripping flesh from prey, strong talons, and their beaks are typically heavier than that of other birds. An eagle's eyes are extremely powerful. An eagle is one of the most dangerous birds in the world, weighing up to 9kg and has a wingspan of 2.5m. An eagle is found near large bodies of water with an abundant food supply and old/broke trees for nesting. For some of us, the anointing that we carry is like the eagle: nothing ordinary or normal. This means that even the journey to get to destiny will never be normal. The stench of the situation that you face can only be solved by the One who allowed it in the first place. Listen, your situation will send for Jesus.

When the disciples heard that Mary had sent for Jesus, their response was that the same Jews who stoned Him now wanted His help (See John 11:8). Maybe it was being said that I rejected Jesus, and now I needed His help. God reached for me from a dead situation. I was being tormented daily by my dead situation in prison, and then God sent His servant to preach the Word. He said the last would be the first (Matthew 20:16), and we know God is God, and He can turn around any situation. You may be at the back of the line, but God will turn it around, and the last will be first. Lazarus was dead, but all Jesus had to say was, "Lazarus, come forth" (See John 11:43), and life returned to the dead.

Can you imagine what that must have been like for Mary, seeing her brother restored? That is how you will feel when Jesus Christ calls you forth out of your dead situation. Your dry bone situation will see life restored to it. These bones will live and be restored. Repeat these words: "I will live again."

The belief I hold is that God placed me in a situation for a purpose. God knows why all the things had happened to me and why I went through the valley of dry bones. He knows my tomorrow. He understands every tear cried, and He understands my worries. It is very encouraging to know that God's delay is not denial of His deliverance and mercy. He hears our daily prayers, and He is an on-time God.

"God, I know You are going to help me. I know You are going to work in my best interest; help me to be patient and strong. "

My mindset changed.

I want to speak into your mind for just a minute. I was in a valley full of other bones like me, with similar situations as mine: dirty, mucky, corrupt, broken, and dead situations. God was right there working out His purposes in the lives of people like me. I know that one day I will be preaching the message to save someone in a dying place.

Looking unto Jesus the author and finisher of our faith; who for the joy that was set before him endured the cross, despising the shame, and is set down at the right hand of the throne of God. (Hebrews 12:2 - KJV).

The Bible says that Jesus Christ endured the cross to become the eternal resurrection (See Hebrews 12:2). I am thirty-seven years old at the writing of this book. I was thirty-six years old when I came into the knowledge, through Jesus Christ, that our mess was necessary to bring God glory. The cross had to happen; the cross was the doorway to life—the cross was where death was conquered. Your mess is a message; your mess can interrupt routines, lifestyles, and everyday movements that keep you at one level. What your mess does is interrupt the cycle that you should be operating in and causes you to stay in seasons way passed the time because your mess makes you oblivious. The mess was designed so that you would be so ashamed that all you want to do with it is cover it up and live a fictitious life that just mirrors real issues. So many people operate out of fear. They behave like an angry bird: unkind and do things that are messed up for people to look at them and think they are the worst. In reality, they are covering up issues they want no one to uncover.

Many women will be in a relationship with more than one partner; you call them a Rahab. They fear being alone; fear being in lack; fear poverty; fear loneliness; fear lack of money, and some fear dealing with mental issues they may have due to situations they went through with rape or molestation. They fear that men do not want them, leading to them living a messy life, not understanding that that mess is really a message. Do you know that people who are messed up have to exhibit strength to constantly carry that mess? Your mess is never light; it is heavy. The reality is, not everyone was designed to carry mess. Not everyone has the backbone to deal with the mess. I can tell you today; you were chosen by God to walk in that mess because you had the ability to become a mess but not only become but overcome it.

There are many people who have lived their lives covering their mess, covering the secret sins, things they cannot tell anyone about because they feel if they expose their mess, it might be used against them. Truth is, they are right. There are many people, according to Nicole Marshall, who are known to be deep-sea divers. These are persons who will never let you move on. They tell everyone your story and try to make you into what you have done. So many people live in fear of exposing their deepest demons, things they have done in the past, and things they struggle with, not knowing these were deliberate. God allowed it, and if God allowed it, there must be a purpose for it.

Many women will never say they have committed abortions, so much so, that they sometimes hear the cries of those babies and cannot sleep. The guilt felt each time they see someone with a child is unbearable. You may be suffering from not being able to get pregnant for your husband because of that abortion that messed up your womb. You feel so guilty but you know if you share your secret with your husband, it may destroy your marriage. Some people are afraid to mention or speak of it because they fear being judged and ostracised by society. Many women like me have had a prison experience but will never speak of it because of what society will say, ignoring or not knowing just how powerful that mess can be for someone else.

I was in a situation where I awoke and saw two persons in a hotel bed with me: a male and a female. I was so drunk, so out of it. I had no idea exactly what transpired; all I knew was that I woke up in a bed with them. That shame and embarrassment was something I could not speak of or tell anyone about. I could not speak of the incident as all I can remember is waking up and seeing them. I have never been attracted to women; never had an experience as an adult with a woman. I do not know what it means to be with a woman. Yet there I was, not knowing how I got myself in that situation. For years, I thought of it but dared not speak of it; I felt dirty. I went in the shower and tried to wash it away, but I could not escape what I woke in, and I did not want to deal with it.

I want you to know that what you try to keep as a secret is what the enemy will use to keep you bound. I remember hearing Evangelist Patricia Perry minister a word: "Shame the devil by talking about the things you have done so he has nothing on you." So many women have been living under the guilt of the abortions committed. It is time to face what you are ashamed of and free yourself of the unnecessary guilt carried because you do not know what is wrapped up in your mess.

Mark 15:34-37 *says, "And at the ninth hour Jesus cried out with a loud voice, saying, "Eloi, Eloi, lama sabachthani?" which is translated, "My God, My God, why have You forsaken Me?" Some of those who stood by, when they heard that, said, "Look, He is calling for Elijah!" Then someone ran and filled a sponge full of sour wine, put it on a reed, and offered it to Him to drink, saying, "Let Him alone; let us see if Elijah will come to take Him down." And Jesus cried out with a loud voice, and breathed His last." (NKJV).*

When Jesus Christ went to the cross, He paid the ultimate price for our sins. The penalty for sin was death, and there was no redemption, but Jesus put an end to that when He echoed, "It is finished." (See John 19:30).

What the enemy meant for evil, God will use to elevate you, if you come into alignment with His principles. If you understand that nothing with God is wasted, you will work the Word. David said in Psalms 139:7-12, *"Where shall I go from your presence, anything I do you are there, anywhere I am you are there." (paraphrased)*. This means when I was committing my mess, God was there and aware of what was happening. What I love about God is that He never leaves your mess. What He does is place His hands upon that mess and cause a divine turnaround so the last can be first, and death will now be life. What we thought was meant to destroy us was really to build us. The mess, after you have accepted it and grown through it, achieving age in it, becomes a message. Your life never stops at the mess; that is where it begins.

For something to be completed, it has to start. Have you ever realised that when a key is placed in a car's ignition, the engine has to turn over for the vehicle to start? When the vehicle starts, it never stays in one position; it drives. But while driving, the vehicle has a destination. The vehicle was not designed to operate on its own; it must have a driver, and in order for the vehicle to move, it must have gasoline. Every process the vehicle undergoes is necessary for it to get to its destination. The greatest thing is: the vehicle does not have to navigate on its own; there is always a driver. Even while you were going through your situation of becoming a mess and being a mess, Jesus Christ was navigating your life the entire time.

"For I know the thoughts that I think toward you, saith the Lord, thoughts of peace, and not evil, to give you an expected end." (Jeremiah 29:11- KJV).

God cannot lie; He is under divine obligation to carry out His Word over your life. Your mess can make normal thinking irrelevant. I learned early on that in the beginning, God—the Creator, the self-existing One, Jehovah, the omnipotent One, omniscient—has our lives in the palm of His hands. If we understand this principle, then we will understand that all things work for our good (See Romans 8:28).

PART II
THE BONES: DEALING WITH ISSUES

CHAPTER 6
ISSUES AND THE SETBACKS

Do not worry about the past or things you cannot change but wish you could: those things that have put you in trouble or turn your life upside down. Instead, be confident and expect great things for your future. Know who you are and Whose you are; know Who holds tomorrow and ensure He holds your hand. I had to be in prison to realise my true calling in Christ Jesus and to settle down and find Him. I had to learn and gain strength.

Currently, you may feel clothed with shame and disgrace but shake off that feeling of the old flesh and enter a new life of love and peace in Jesus Christ.

My setbacks were a set up for my deliverance and blessings from God. I received deliverance from chains, bondage, sin, depression and so many more unspeakable things. There were issues only God could remove. When I was sent to prison, it was not a setback, it was a set up for blessing and restoration; no more wailing, depression, and failures. I am not dead; I am alive and much stronger than before. I wrote sections of this book from behind prison walls. This valley experience is one of the best experiences of my life.

You have been marked for destruction, but God has destined you for greatness, and it does not matter what you have gone through in the past; the bad decisions you made, the mess you created, or the destruction you called on yourself. Once you turn your life over to Jesus Christ, the Bible says, *"Therefore if any man be in Christ, he is a new creature: old things have passed away; all things are become new."* (2 Corinthians 5:7). We all have a future, but the type of future we have solely depends on God. However, we all have a past, and, many times, our past is not pretty. It is often filled with many issues, pain, heartbreak, failures, depression, and the list continues. I often wondered why persons garden-trim the old leaves for fresh leaves to grow. This is similar to us when God has to strip us of baggage in our lives so His purpose can spring forth into our lives and give us a brighter and more fulfilling future with God.

In my years of existence—twenty-seven years old when I was in prison—I had so many issues, only God could have kept me alive. I struggled with heavy depression for over ten years; the worst part of it was before being taken to prison. I lost a job I had for over eight years; lost benefits I was highly anticipating; lost my grandfather, and lost my best friend, Michelle. All these bad things happened to me without a reason why. I had men break me up on the inside for reasons I can never properly explain. I lost everything I had built. The sacrifices I had to make were so huge, so hurtful, and so hard that I felt like Job at one point. I did not have peace within. I could not even take care of my first child the way I wanted to because I had so much going on. I felt like I was not a mother, and he deserved more. That little boy was one of the most precious gifts God has ever given me, until I was given two little angels.

As an antidote for the pain I was feeling, I ended up putting tattoos on my body and doing body piercings. The tattoos were signs, symbols of events, and special things in my life, but they did not matter after a while. I wanted them gone. Friends, or those I called friends, even family I had trusted and opened up to, gave everything to, were only there to take whatever they could. There was no loyalty. The dreams I had were shelved because of devastating circumstances; my life was a huge mess. I had nothing positive to look forward to at the time, except being medicated by anti-depressants and falling asleep.

I remember a situation that occurred in my life where after I walked away from a committed relationship I had for over six years and borne a child from, I got involved with another man. This man became aware of my circumstances and decided to use the situation to the best of his abilities and gain whatever he could. I fell for all his tricks and deceit. I was used and then thrown away like garbage after he had benefited and acquired all he wanted.

Honestly, I did not know I could have recovered from everything that happened; it was too much to deal with. The heartbreak could not be explained to anyone because I felt so stupid and ashamed: the deceit, lies, and, worst of all, the huge set up that took place. I felt like I was destroyed on the inside and would never be able to trust anyone ever again. I told myself that I hated men, and I was going to give up on friendships and ever having another relationship, but that is a lie from the pit of hell. My depression and addiction to anti-depressants were the enemy's window of opportunity to do so many things to me. I was robbed, not just of valuables, but of my innocence, trust, knowledge, and so much more. I gave people everything because they said they loved me, and I was never told that by anyone. When I was told they would stand by me and help, I thought God had sent His angels. The man I was with before prison made me feel like I could do what I wanted once the money was right.

Listen, when you are in trouble, all you want to hear is that someone has your back and loves you no matter what. They only need to utter what you want to hear, and, after a time, you become vulnerable to that person. Even if you know that person is not yours, once you are made to feel that you are, you open yourself to so much that will hurt you in the long run. This man abused me, not physically—my mama did not raise a fool—but I was an emotional wreck. I did not think I could get over it. Maybe the situation hurt so badly due to the level of trust I placed in this man. I did not think I could let go. I honestly thought I would die.

All these unfortunate circumstances had to happen—nothing just happens—it was all ordained by God to happen. Maybe you had similar experiences. Read carefully, "Do not let your past hold you back from the great future that Jesus Christ has for you." When you accept Jesus Christ into your life as Lord and Saviour, and He becomes part of your new life, it should not matter who has hurt, used, abused, or done you wrong. When you take Jesus Christ, old wounds of the past become irrelevant and non-existent. God did not take you to the mountain top for you to concentrate on the valley. He took you to the mountain and out of the valley for you to be highly lifted. My mother, sisters, and daughters, if you could get a glimpse of how God sees you in heaven, you would not burden yourself with unnecessary, depressing memories. Dare to be a daughter of Zion. Dare to be a daughter of Abraham: full of faith, determined to make it through any circumstance. Be an Esther, the Queen. Know what you are capable of and the power you hold inside of you; know you are a child of the King and you are beautiful. Look at yourself as a vessel of honour, not to be used by men, but by God Almighty. You are a vessel of honour with a beautiful mind, and you are flawless in every area of your life. You are not to be taken advantage of by men; take advantage of the fact that you are a princess, Daddy's little girl, who only has great things in store for your life. The men who have come and gone, let them go with whatever they took. When things are taken away from us, know that God is a God who restores to His children a double portion.

For those who still desire a husband, tell your heavenly Father, "I do not only want to be blessed with a husband; I want to be highly favoured with a good husband who knows the love of God, who can love me the way God intended for man to love his wife." Ladies, you are more than your hips and thighs. You are beautiful inside and out and you are blessed.

"For I know the thoughts that I think toward you, saith the Lord, thoughts of peace, and not of evil, to give you an expected end." (Jeremiah 29:11).

CHAPTER 7
THE COFFIN THAT COULD NOT CLOSE

The enemy tried everything to kill my purpose. The truth is, I was actually dead because I fell into the trap and died due to a lack of knowledge of whom I was and where I was going. I had done so many things, fell into so many different situations that disqualified me in the eyes of man. This is how we truly know and understand the Scriptures that says if God be for us, who can be against us (Romans 8:31).

Roman 8:35-39 helps us understand how much God loves us. This Scripture explains God's immeasurable love and God's compassionate attribute towards us (Professor Miguel Smith).

*"Who shall separate us from the love of Christ? Shall tribulation, or distress, or persecution, or famine, or nakedness, or peril, or sword? As it is written: "For Your sake we are killed all day long; we are accounted as sheep for the slaughter." Yet in all these things we are more than conquerors through Him who loved us. For I am persuaded that neither death nor life, nor angels nor principalities nor powers, nor things present nor things to come, nor height nor depth, nor any other created thing, shall be able to separate us from the love of God which is in Christ Jesus our Lord." (*Romans 8:35-39 – NKJV).

I remember a Sunday School in October 2019, Pastor Dean Smith of Light of the Gentile International Ministries, who is also the shepherd God has placed over my life, was doing a session with us. He went in-depth on God's love, and he said something that brought me back to this very period in my life that I am writing about. It gave me a perfect understanding of why the enemy could not bury me. He said: "We have the privilege to call God 'daddy' as we are seated in heavenly places." He went on to explain that nothing can separate us from the love of God; He is just a "Daddy call" away. Once we understand the fullness of God's love, we will understand who we are. His resurrection power overrules all plans and death traps of the enemy.

So many events have happened. Looking back today, it must have been over ten thousand angels on guard for me not to die. I remember going to parties at 12 AM, drinking, raving, and having fun until 8 AM. I was loaded with pills, alcohol, and weed; all to get me high. I went behind the wheel to drive myself to any destination I wanted to go, yet I never encountered an accident, not even hitting a dog. The songwriter, Cory Ashbury, says: "Oh the overwhelming, never-ending reckless love of God." There have been battles won on my behalf that I did not even know about.

The state of my life, where I was and who I had become, was conducive to death. It had everything that attracted death; it even opened the door. Death was never my portion as God had spoken what my portion was. There is something we need to understand, even reading this book, that our lives are in the palm of His hands. Once we are in the palm, our lives have to take the direction God has ordained for us. The grave could not close because the love of God is never-ending concerning my life, and that continues to give me life, even after being dead, after the many afflictions and the assassination attempts of the enemy.

I had so many issues, unanswered questions, hurt, pain, and heartbreak. The fact is, I was already imprisoned in my mind even before I arrived at a physical prison. I felt like I did not have hope or anything to live for; I wanted to die and forget about everything and everyone. There was no question in my mind that I was being tormented by depression. I wanted to cry, but the tears would not come; enough was not inside to come out. I felt naked and ashamed. I did not know myself; I was trying to hide, and I could not. So, I told myself that suicide was the only way to get out of what I was going through.

Suicide apparently hated me, for some strange reason. I tried to be its friend on numerous occasions, doing what it required, with all the pills, overdosing with alcohol, careless and reckless driving; nothing worked. I remember I was living in an apartment in Oaklands, and there was a day I did not want to face this life anymore. Everything I had tried to leave was just not working. I heard a voice telling me to try jumping through the window. I had about thirty pills; I remember swallowing some with alcohol. I did everything in my will to jump through that window, but all that happened was me falling asleep for days, waking in tears to the reality that I was still alive; crying, "God, why are you tormenting me? I want to die. I cannot live this life anymore." This life, to me, had no meaning, no sense; I was just a mess with no hope of ever getting better.

I had nothing to my name; everything was taken from me. All I owned was what I had in the car while going to court and the clothes on my back. Everything else was taken from me: my home, business, money, clothes, shoes, jewelry; all of it was stolen right in front of me, and I could not do anything about it. The worst part was, I had lost my mind and who I was created to be. Mental health is the biggest battle one will ever face in this life. I was so far gone in my mind that there was absolutely no hope of coming back, much less redemption. Our thoughts are not God's thoughts; neither are our ways God's ways (See Isaiah 58:9).

"Then shall thy light break forth as the morning, and thine health shall spring forth speedily: and thy righteousness shall go before thee; the glory of the Lord shall be thy reward. Then shalt thou call, and the Lord shall answer; thou shalt cry, and he shall say, Here I am, If thou take away from the midst of thee the yoke, the putting forth of the finger, and speaking vanity." (Isaiah 58:8-9).

"Come now, and let us reason together, saith the Lord: though your sins be as scarlet, they shall be as white as snow; though they be red like crimson, they shall be as wool." (Isaiah 1:18).

"Likewise the Spirit also helpeth our infirmities: for we know not what we should pray for as we ought: but the Spirit itself maketh intercession for the saints according to the will of God." (Romans 8:26).

The Lord blew my mind with these three Scriptures. The thoughts I had about myself were not the thoughts of God towards me. He had a far better and greater plan for my life. I thought I was so far gone I wanted to die, but God had a different plan. He wanted to make a difference in my life. There is a song that says: "When He was on the cross, I was on His mind." I know I was on His mind as God has proven to me that the viler the sinner, the richer the glory. In that season of my life, the Lord showed me that the setbacks were preparations for a greater comeback. This was a comeback that would nullify every assignment of the enemy; a comeback that would not only affect my life, but affect the lives of all I would come across and share my testimony with. It perfectly describes my life when the Scripture says all things work together for the good of God and all those that are called to His purpose (Romans 8:28).

The Lord opened my eyes in that season of my life when I was broken and showed me that He could give me an encounter and change my entire life forever. He showed me that death was necessary for resurrection. Many people die simple deaths because they were created to be simple, but there are those of us who have to bear a heavy cross because of what has been placed upon us.

The ministry that is inside of you will attract the same level of warfare; every struggle that you face, every mess you encounter is an indication of the ministry that is on your life.

If I was "okay," I would not need a doctor. If a pregnant woman does not feel labour pains, then she would not know it is time for the doctor to deliver that baby. What God did was allow the entire chaos of my existence, so I would be broken; I was dead for Him to step in and give me a new life.

It took me reaching that state of decomposition for God to begin to minister to me. He allowed me to see that all other options had failed, and He was the only solution. God made sure I was at a stage in my life where everything I valued had failed me, and He was the only One who could get the glory. God stepped in at a time when all I could do was totally surrender.

Isaiah 40:8 says, *"The grass withereth, the flower fadeth: but the word of our God shall stand for ever."*

The Word God spoke and declared over your life is forever, and it cannot be rendered null and void. Everything around you will be for a season and fade away, but the Word of God over your life is eternal. My situations and circumstances could not dictate my future; it was the Word that had the final say. It was a Word why drugs, suicide, depression, and even prison could not take me out. It was the Word why prison could not be my final destination. It is the Word why I am able to write this book to you today, telling you that because of the Word: "Failure is not final, victory is!"

My Prison Break

The Word God planted in you from before He even formed you in your mother's womb has a dominating effect; it overrides everything else and remains standing forever. The Word that is inside you will disrupt what you considered your norm and bring you into God's reality for your life. The Word provides information about you from God and gives you the ammunition to go forth and recover. This is why one of the enemy's weapons is to keep your mind in bondage because once you get a hint of who you are, it will cause you to become hungry for more. Once you taste a bit of who you truly are, it will ignite your curiosity, and you will begin to seek. It was the Word that was over my life why I could not die, and the coffin that was prepared for me that I even went and laid in could not close.

I started praying differently after my encounter with God; it was no longer: "God, please let me go home" but "Lord, please keep me in here and transform me, then when I am ready, send me home to my new life on the outside."

I understood Isaiah 43 and what God was saying about me:

"But now thus saith the Lord that created thee, O Jacob, and he that formed thee, O Israel, Fear not: for I have redeemed thee, I have called thee by thy name; thou art mine. When thou passest through the waters, I will be with thee; and through the rivers, they shall not overflow thee: when thou walkest through the fire, thou shalt not be burned; neither shall the flame kindle upon thee. For I am the Lord thy God, the Holy One of Israel, thy Saviour: I gave Egypt for thy ransom, Ethiopia and Seba for thee. Since thou wast precious in my sight, thou hast been honourable, and I have loved thee: therefore will I give men for thee, and people for thy life."

There is something inside of you, and God will not let it die. In fact, God is attracted to what is inside of you. He can identify with what is on the inside of you. No matter how far gone you think you are in this life, even when you have forgotten God, what is inside of you cannot make Him forget you. This is why David asked, "Where can I go from Your presence?" (See Psalms 139:7-12).

Genesis 2:7, *"And the LORD God formed man of the dust of the ground, and breathed into his nostrils the breath of life; and man became a living soul."*

What caused the life? God spoke (See Genesis 1:1-3). What did He speak? He spoke the Word. His Word brings life. When you speak a Word, breath comes forth. The Scripture also informs us that Word is spirit and power (See 1 Thessalonians 1:5). Amen. When God was forming you, He planted a word that would give you life and bring back life inside of others. He will not let it die. What is the Word? The Scripture says in John 1:1, *"In the beginning was the word and the word was with God and the word was God."*

God gave you a piece of Himself, and He cannot die. This means that He must come for you by any means necessary. This is why you cannot die a victim and a slave to circumstances.

He sent Moses for Israel because He had promised Abraham concerning his generation. No matter how the children of Israel rebelled and sinned, their cry reminded God of His covenant with their forefather, Abraham. The piece of Himself that He had given to Abraham was His Word, and God will never deny His Word.

God sent His only Son for His chosen and the illegal aliens, the Gentiles, so all could be saved. He sent Jesus to create a way, so He could always have access, and sin could no longer block Him. He shed His blood. This blood gave us access, but that is not the main thing. The bigger picture was God having unlimited access to man because now His Spirit was able to live inside of us, to guide, teach, and protect us. Jesus went seeking the lost because He had an investment to collect on.

CHAPTER 8
ABORT THE ABORTION

When I found out I was still pregnant with my son, the young prophet, the enemy tried everything and anything he could for that child not to come to full term. I had so many experiences that pronounced death, but all I could see was life and a child surviving despite the odds. I remember when I was in prison, my mother came to visit and brought items. When I was going to see her, I remember feeling out of it. When I came to myself, I was in an ambulance. I had fallen and hit my stomach and head. Everyone was worried, thinking that was the end of my pregnancy. To our surprise, my child and I were fine.

The devil tried to sabotage my pregnancy again when I was seven months pregnant; this was one evening after lockdown. I was experiencing pains, but they were not strong. After lockdown, everyone was reading or doing things to keep occupied and focused, trying to keep their head above water. I remember having pain, but they were on and off; fifteen minutes apart, and then they began to come more frequently. In my first pregnancy, which was carried full term, I was not in labour, so I had no clue what it felt like to be in labour. I was not aware that I was in early labour. I remember the pain intensifying, and I cried for help. The pain was so bad, I was motionless. I felt my pelvis contracting, and that was when I realised something was wrong. The pain was so bad, I gave a loud shout. The ladies in the dorm began to call the officers working the night shift to get the nurse on duty. Other persons started looking for their best clothes and towels to pack a bag as they were saying I was in labour and had nothing to wear.

I remember a lady who became my prison mom; I will not mention her name, as she may not want me to. She was serving a life sentence, and she went to her section at the back and took her best towels, nightgown, and panties and placed in a bag. I remember her saying she was getting a grandchild. May God bless her soul for being so kind to someone she hardly knew. May God favour her for her kindness and compassion shown to me.

The pains intensified, and I felt like I was going to blackout. I remember whispering, "Lord, help me." There was a Christian lady in the dorm who started to pray. I remember other prisoners also joining in prayer; it was like Pentecost. They began quoting Scriptures, and as they were praying, I felt the baby turn and return to his original position in the womb to await the nine months. That day, the prayers of inmates who knew and understood God's power aborted the enemy's attempts.

There was another attempt when I was almost nine months pregnant. I woke up, not feeling well. The pregnancy had become so heavy, and my legs and back were heavy with the weight. I remember walking to the kitchen where the daily supper was being prepared. As I approached the door, the next thing I knew, I was being pushed in a wheelbarrow to the area called the surgery: the sickbay. I was told by my fellow inmates that I had fallen on my belly. There was a doctor on duty that day who attended to me after the fall and said I was fine.

There were so many experiences where I felt or just had unfortunate circumstances that wanted me to deliver this child before time or try to assassinate the pregnancy. However, once again, God reinforced that purpose cannot hide. The conditions to have a child in prison were not the most favourable, but prayer can change any atmosphere and any situation. I remember talking to God and telling Him, "Give me peace in all of this." I realised that I was not going to get bail so I needed to settle in my mind where I was going to have my child. I was told to be at peace and allow God to carry out His will, and that is exactly what I did.

On August 17, 2010 I gave birth to a beautiful baby boy at the Spanish Town Hospital in St. Catherine. I delivered via a C-Section. I was taken in by officers in sets of two for each shift; they changed shifts three times daily. I went into the operating theatre at 10 AM and was given an anesthetic to sleep through the process. When I awoke, I could not tell the time or anything; all I wanted to know was where my baby was. All I wanted to do was look at him; I was now given a second chance as a mother.

When I became pregnant, I did not want the baby because the situation was not right. I had gotten pregnant for a man who was married with a family. He was a friend and comfort before I started sleeping with him. I had developed an attachment to him for the gratification of flesh, not for a baby. When I found out I was pregnant in November 2009, I told him I wanted an abortion. He did not disagree. Can I tell you that for some strange reason, I hoped he would say no: shame on me. He actually gave me the money needed to proceed with the abortion. I went ahead and took what I needed to take for the baby to bleed out. This is without knowing that the prophetic word had already taken root inside my womb.

Friend, the Word of God says: "Purpose cannot die." (Psalms 118:17). My son is living proof that this is so because I took everything necessary to get rid of him. I used to feel ashamed to even share with anyone that I tried to do an abortion; it would not have been my first abortion. I had many, including trying to abort my own purpose. I remember after I was incarcerated and found out I was still pregnant, I had questions: "How is this possible? What am I going to do? How am I going to get out of this one?" But who cared about how I felt? The Word of God over your life overrules and overrides everything concerning your life. If God says you shall live, then you cannot die.

There are many women out there today who are faced with the same unbearable challenges that I was faced with. If you are afraid to carry a child because it will be too embarrassing for you, especially if you are in church and the shame would be too much, let me encourage you today, sister, "Carry your baby." This situation was not an easy one, and, in my mind, nothing good could come from it. In fact, the word 'good' was not even considered when I thought about this baby but look what the Lord has done. Today I look at my boys, and I give God glory for their lives because only God could have done this.

Many of us also aborted the mission and dropped the baby God had given us to carry because of the pressures that the ministry comes with. The enemy has not made it easy because the ministry you carry will shift regions or affect continents. Today, I encourage you to abort the abortion procedure, go back and hold your position. If God places it inside of you, He will see you through until the end.

PART III
HEALED AND BE MADE WHOLE

CHAPTER 9
THE BIGGER PRISON

In July 2011, I started serving my ten-year prison sentence. I had gotten to a stage where I came face-to-face with my natural life and wanted to have a fresh start. I pleaded guilty to all charges and accepted all my wrongs. This is also the time I started the eternal sentence with Jesus Christ. I was baptised and fully committed my life to God. A week before my baptism, I sent my son home to be with my mother until my sentence was over.

Starting the sentence with Christ was where the dead weight was shed, and the true me came to life. This was where I faced the issues dead on, even those I did not want to deal with, in order to receive total deliverance and healing. Acknowledging the issues and receiving Christ was just the start of the journey, but there was a bigger picture. Even though I was now sentenced in a physical prison to serve time set by man, I was wrapped in a mental prison way before I was sentenced to that physical prison. Accepting Jesus Christ was now the journey to become free. This was where I would face my demons, past issues and come to be set free.

While incarcerated, the Lord used the time to teach me servanthood and obedience. I found joy in cleaning the church and being an orderly to the Chaplin, which was my first ministry. I had peace knowing that God had loved me so much to grant me a second chance, even in prison.

My Prison Break

In 2014, as I served and honoured the Lord in my prison situation, the Lord decided to favour me. The prison had a special Easter service put on by a non-profit organization. They carried a special speaker: a lady pastor. When I met this lady, it was one of those unforgettable experiences. She gave me a message from the Lord; she said I should go on a three-day Esther fast. This fast was God stretching me. This was new to me: something I did not know existed, and something I did not think could be done. I was obedient when the Lord said to do it without water or food, and the Holy Spirit carried me through. After going on the fast, I was awarded parole; my sentence was cut short, and I was home in 2014, which was way before my release date.

The Sunday before I left prison, I preached my first message at the pulpit. The message was titled: "Take me to the King."

I had an encounter as I was taken to the King, and this is where the Lord showed me that I had to start from the beginning to receive the real Prison Break. One of the first things the Lord did for me was to explain the gift of salvation that I had received while I was still incarcerated. He wanted me to fully understand what a life in Christ meant, and so the journey began. The gift of salvation for me was that I was no longer indebted to the enemy for the sins of my past or even the present. I understood that Jesus had purchased my life with His blood, and He was now responsible for Stacy-Ann Garvey. It meant that God was now putting everything in my life in order and teaching me that I was no longer in charge, but He is in charge of my life. My only responsibility was obedience to God. The Lord showed me that of self, I was not able to do it. I would fail and come to nothing, as I was inadequate. But being obedient to God through Jesus Christ would cause me to achieve complete deliverance and move forward in my new life. What God required was my obedience to the Holy Spirit's leading and being truthful to myself to break free from my mental prison.

Every heart needs a specific diagnosis as every heart has a different story. You cannot make mistakes with the truth, as all the truth can be is the truth. In order for you to get the actual diagnosis to heal your heart, it requires your truth. I decided to face my truth for God to solve my problems. One of the truths is: there was nothing "good" about me.

I sat for months, trying to decide how I was going to face my truth and tell my story. I tried to reason with God about how I would even start telling my story; it was agonisingly painful and hard to face. There is so much to face, yet so much I wished I would never have to tell. My story is filled with so much pain, hurt, and sorrow. It would even be embarrassing at some points, but God allowed me to understand that it is my truth; a truth that He will use for His kingdom.

I always knew I was different growing up; I did not do anything average. I always pursued things I believed in, always had my own opinions, and, yes, I was as stubborn as they come. I did not look like the rest of my family; I was re-skinned with brown eyes, which highlighted me as a feisty little girl. I grew up with my grandparents for most of my years, and they were never the grandparents to say "I love you," but their actions showed it.

I grew up in a family that was Christian-oriented, but no one was a Christian. My parents, aunts, and uncles were always partying and drinking; my grandmother was the only one basically in church. I was not always raised in the church. When I lived with my mother, who always had bars and restaurants, I knew about partying and drinking alcohol, not because she was a bad mother, but because that is the life she knew. I started doing my own partying during my teenage years, but it was mild. I then did more partying when I was with my first son's father; he had a club, and he loved to party. After I started going through the heavy depression, I realized that partying and alcohol were an antidote, and that was when it became a lifestyle.

I was in church at the time to please my grandmother. I was always active in youth fellowship and somehow developed this big dream to become a pastor one day, so it made sense to keep that church image and not do anything wrong. There was always something inside of me that I could not explain to anyone; it felt like there was more to church than just the same things I kept seeing repeatedly. During my teenage years, I grew up between my grandparents and mother. At age sixteen, I started having feelings and curiosity about my body and life, but there was no one to talk to. Television and soap operas only showed people in relationships and drama with no real explanations about anything. Yet, my desire for what I was seeing was real, and I could not help it. I was searching because I knew something was missing from my life, and in searching, I realised that I had never been loved. With the back and forth between my mother and grandparents, I was frustrated and empty at that time.

I realised that my body had changed; my features were becoming noticeable, like what I was seeing in the movies. I began to desire what curious teenagers desired: a boyfriend, because that is where love seemed to come from and, oh yes, I got one for sure. I met my first crush and love interest in High School, but I did not know what to do or how to be a girlfriend. I also ended up moving away from where I was living, so the relationship never materialised the way it would have if I had stayed.

At sixteen years old, I went back to live with my grandparents. I met and fell deep and far in love quickly and dangerously with my first boyfriend while going to church as a young Christian, and we had a full-fledge relationship. It got to a stage where I started compromising my body and having sex with the young man who I loved and thought loved me just as much, and who I thought would make me his wife. I did not want to lose the relationship; it was my everything. I gave in to having sex with him because he told me that all his friends were doing it and he felt left out. After having sex for the first time with him, I remember being told that he did not feel that my body was that of a virgin, and I did not bleed like most girls. I was never told that I should bleed; I was so in love that I made sure I did.

I started being disrespected by him after giving him my body. The treatment got worst, but I was in love, so I held on. Rejection can cause you to receive things from people that you really should not; the pain of rejection is too much, so you think it is better to stay because you tell yourself that you would rather this than being alone. There were times in the relationship where the wounds of words felt like a gunshot. I did not know just how horrible being cheated on could make you feel. I had seen it in soap operas, but the reality was a whole other ball game. It hurts worse than hell and can destroy you in an instant.

I remember doing my first abortion when I was eighteen years old. I thought the relationship we had would last forever, and I did not want to mess up his life, so we did what we thought was best when I got pregnant. I was working for a very reputable organization. I started there at age eighteen through the HEART Trust SL-TOPS program. I did well, and favour was also on my life as the company kept me. After being at the company for years, you would see things and thought that going against a company policy to assist customers was okay because other workers were doing it.

I had just started working, and he was in college, so to make life "better" for both of us, we decided to abort the pregnancy. He followed me to do it but left me to bear all the pain; it was okay because I was in love. I carried that pain for years; it was hard to forget. I remember what I went through and could not explain to anyone just how ashamed I was. My mind experienced its first trauma that numbed parts of me, making me silent. After leaving college, he went into the army, and I was so excited for him. The dream of being married and having a family was all I could think of. I was very close to his family as I grew up in their eyes; we all went to the same church. All that was on my mind and heart was that he promised to marry me, and that was heaven for me at eighteen years old.

I remember buying myself an engagement ring and engaging myself to the man who was never engaged to me. He left for training in England and, months after, I realised that he left me too. I prayed morning, noon, and night for my marriage to him to become a reality. I prayed that he would call me. I prayed that he would come back to me. He left me, and I was in the dark with no switch to turn on the lights.

I ended up being left in the dark after he went into the army, and it became obvious that I did not fit his lifestyle anymore. This was the first time a man was leaving me, and this was the first time I experienced depression. This was where my problems got worse. I had struggled with rejection all my life, and now depression was added to the mix, and things started getting worst. I had now become this broken little girl with shattered dreams, who had no daddy to run into his arms and cry. I had loved this guy so much, and suffering this loss was truly devastating. All of this happened, and my family had no idea. Funny thing is, I think they did know, even though my family was seriously disconnected.

For months I sat around waiting for him to reach out and say, "Let's start over," but nothing. I became ill without realising; it was not just a physical illness, but my mental health was now off. This was the first time I started taking medical drugs to combat depression. It helped, but it did not help. I needed more; I needed a cure for the pain, so I started going out with a friend, and that is how I met my first son's father; in the same year my relationship ended. I fell into his arms and quickly succumbed to love again as that was what I thought it was. I entered this relationship to soothe wounds from the old as well as to feel loved. He did just that, and it consumed me and turned me into a monster-in-love. I did not know love could break out old wounds and make them fester so badly. I did not know love could send you into the hospital for stress and depression. I was a broken hazard to him and to myself.

I became a housewife to a man who, at that time, was not looking for a wife. I loved this man so much that my entire life revolved around him. I would be at his beck and call. I cooked his dinner, cleaned the house the way he liked, fixed the house to make it as comfortable as possible for him, and everything that a good wife would do to keep him because I just could not lose again. He knew just how to keep me running after him.

There were times when we were happy, and there were times when he would be a husband to me. But the demons that tormented his life just would not leave, so nothing with us would last. He seemed to love me, but the full commitment and marriage were not coming. Each time I got pregnant, I had to abort the baby, and the cheating kept getting worse. The anger got so horrible, I started being physically violent with him. I did not know love could put you in the hospital for treatment.

CHAPTER 10
THE ANALYSIS

Forgiveness

It should be noted that I had a lawyer prior to me going into prison. I told him about the pregnancy a month before the abortion, trying to get out of a court appearance. He was not aware I had aborted the baby, so he had them note that I was pregnant on the court documents. When I got to the hospital, the prison informed them that I was pregnant based on the court documents that came with me when I was taken there.

I spent all day at the hospital with officers guarding me and, later that evening, I was returned to prison. Upon returning, reality hit on just how badly I messed up my life. Wishing I could turn back the hands of time was just circling in my head, but that is all it could do: circle in my head. The following day I got up and tried to find a way to get myself out of the mess. It was not working; it would not come my direction. I tried to strike a plea bargain with the devil, but not even the devil wanted to look in my direction. I guess I was already such a mess; there was nothing for him to mess up.

After carefully examining my life through the lens of the Holy Spirit, I identified my problems. These were problems that would not take a one-time fix but a continuous walk with God and staying in the palm of His hands. I began to write letters to God because I needed a change. The first letter I wrote to God was for Him to teach me how to forgive. This came with much fasting and prayer. I did not even want to hear the word 'forgiveness' when I realised all the hurt I had been carrying all these years because of what people have done and said about me, or even what was not done to me. I was hesitant to forgive; I did not understand the power of forgiveness. A mistake we make as children of God is thinking forgiveness benefits others more than us. The truth is, forgiveness does more good for us than those we are forgiving. Apart from setting our heart free, it opens the door for joy, peace, and love, which is the Holy Spirit.

Think of it this way: if God did not forgive us, where would we be? God forgives our trespasses so we can forgive those who trespass against us (Matthew 6:14). What a powerful statement. In 2018, I attended a conference called "Weeping, Wailing, Worshipping Women." One of the things that was at the forefront of the conference was confronting our issues. What it did was to allow persons to come face to face with their issues and taught them the power of forgiveness. How will forgiveness set you free? The first person I had to forgive was myself. I had to forgive myself for disappointing myself, forgive myself for the embarrassment of being a bad mother, the careless life I lived, abortions, the crime I committed, and everyone I had caused hurt. I had to forgive myself and then accept that God had forgiven me. I wrote a letter to myself outlining everything that I ever did; all I could remember. I even wrote in the letter the mistakes I may make in the future. I wrote that it was all paid for by the blood of Jesus. I took my mind to the place where Christ made a sacrifice for my life, and I accepted this sacrifice. In accepting that sacrifice, I forgave myself. This led me on a journey where I began to forgive all I could remember, after forgiving myself. Sometimes, even after going through all that, hidden things will leave a residue in our hearts.

In June 2006, after a five-year relationship, I found out that I was pregnant with my first son, and I made up my mind to keep the baby. I had already committed four or six abortions in my twenty-four years of life, and I was tired of doing what the man in my life wanted me to do and not what Stacy-Ann wanted. I was tired of doing something I knew was wrong just to keep my relationship. I was so in love with having what I craved, which was love, that I would do just about anything.

When I found out that I was pregnant this time, I had decided no more abortions. He told me he was not ready for a baby after years of being together, and he would leave me if I went through with the pregnancy. I went through with the pregnancy, and he moved out of the house where we lived together. During my pregnancy, I carried a baby as a first-time mother by myself. There were occasions he would call and check on me. Occasionally, he would come with me to the doctor's visit. When the ultrasound revealed that it was a boy, his attitude changed. He started coming to see me, but he would not stay. He would take me to get stuff for the baby. He was there for his son's birth and was very excited as our son was born a few hours before his birthday. This book is not to discredit him as a father; I will be the first to say that he has been a great father to his son.

I never told anyone about this experience. I lied about it and kept the real truth hidden for almost a decade and a half. I was about twenty-three years old when I got pregnant for the fourth or fifth time. This was before the pregnancy I brought to term and delivered my son. I remember at about four or five months into the pregnancy, I was at work and I lied to everyone about how happy I was and how the father was thrilled. I was too ashamed to tell them the truth: that a man I lived with for years walked out on me because I decided to carry his baby. I had sleepless nights, and because I did not want to harm the baby, I could not take the anti-depressants, so my nights were turmoil. I realised that sinus tablets helped me sleep, so I started taking those to help, but only for a minute. I could not handle the loneliness or depression. Each day got worse for me mentally. I started thinking that maybe keeping the baby was a mistake.

Looking back, one of the things I realised is that my relationship was a drug for me: a pill that I believed made me better but, the truth is, it was making me ill. As things got worst mentally, I became sick physically, and demons started plaguing me. I then desired to be in a hospital as the spirits started to say it would cause my baby father to feel sorry for me and sympathise and come back to me. Daily I desired to end up in the hospital until I actually ended up there. Being in the hospital did cause him to come see me. While traveling home from the hospital, the internal conversation was about getting rid of the pregnancy to fix our relationship. Thinking of the pain I was already facing on my own, and how unbearable the depression was, I decided I would do it.

I remember waking up the morning, rubbing my belly at almost five months with a guilt that was bigger than my actual belly. I kept trying to console my conscience that had started counting the abortions that I had already done. My body was already tired of doing DNCs; I had seen enough being pulled out of my body but I said this was the last one just to save my relationship and cure me of the mental illness inside of me.

I went into the doctor's office, took my clothes off, and laid on the bed. I had never felt so cold and numb in my entire life. I knew I should not be in there, and I could feel my heart saying, "Stacy-Ann, no," but rejection kept reminding me that I had a relationship to save and not lose again.

The doctor came in and started the most painful process in my soberness. I saw the baby get pulled out of me, and I was so dead and powerless to stop what I was doing to myself and to another life. "*How could God create a monster like me?"* I thought. I saw everything, but all I could do was lay there as a precious life that came out of me was lying in a basin just asking me why.

I got it together and went home, and took some drugs to sleep for days; it was the same routine, until one day I broke. I was not sleeping properly because the images would not leave my mind. The sound of babies crying was tormenting me. My health started deteriorating until I became seriously, mentally ill. Suicide now located me and gave me the formula to try and kill myself. I tried but failed at the attempts as someone always kept finding me.

The spirit of abortion entered my life at the age of eighteen, and was determined to stay. This is why I encourage women not to give in; yes, it is your body, and you do have a right, but the spiritual aspects of abortion are far more long-lasting and dangerous than a DNC. This affects your entire life's purpose and dreams. This spirit will cause you to miscarry when it comes to breakthroughs, and the spirit of "almost" will be on your life. You will always be saying, "I almost got it," but you never will. For years, even after being a Christian, I had many near breakthroughs, but it would never happen for me until I received deliverance from the spirit of abortion.

Things looked like they were coming together with my child's father for a month after my son was born, but nothing changed; things got worse. My depression got worst, and I had to receive medical attention. I started to get dependent on sleeping pills to get numb. I was facing postpartum depression, along with depression that I had been suffering from before. I was now a perfect mess. The worst part was: there were so many people around, but no one could help me. No one knew how or what was happening to me. They were blinded by the facade I put on. I looked good; I was always on a high when they saw me, living my best life, the person everyone came to for everything—what a deception. I was a hot mess, rotting away. I needed help.

The residue can multiply, and this multiplication can leave scars we do not want to deal with because it hurts too much. However, today, I can encourage you that the scars are not meant to be permanent, but they will hurt if you do not clean and medicate the wound. The first step to your healing is facing the truth, opening up, and then asking for help from the Holy Spirit. That is how the healing begins. Today, the Holy Spirit still reminds me of areas in my life where I need to heal or areas I had not dealt with. As the Holy Spirit reminds me, I move in obedience. I could only write this book as I forgave myself and others and allowed the Lord to use all of this to help anyone who will read this.

That is a scar I carried for almost eighteen years. I got delivered from that scar in 2017 when the Holy Spirit allowed me to attend a conference called "Woman Stay Loosed" that focused on us facing and dealing with the issues, learning, and forgiveness. I had been so in love with my child's father that I continued in a relationship when I was the only one in it: no love or respect; there was nothing.

It is more powerful to forgive than hold on to the baggage. The healing is more powerful than the issue faced. The healing has more impact than the scars. People will remember your issues, but they will acknowledge and honor you based on the healing that cannot be hidden and causes you to excel.

Rejection

Rejection is a powerful thing. Many of us miss it because we do not understand the power of rejection. We fail to realise that the most famous people in the world also have stories of rejection. The most famous person to walk this earth was Jesus; He came and His own rejected Him. I have come to understand that many will reject what they cannot contain. Many of us were never built to be enclosed in a box; we were made to conquer and empower. The plan of the enemy is to shut us down before we realise this about ourselves. Many do not realise this until it is too late; however, it is better late than never. I remember hearing a powerful word from Reverend T.D. Jakes: "Rejected But Still Blessed."

One thing that is most powerful—I hope this sticks in your mind forever—is that those who are rejected were divinely selected by God. Let us use the story of David in 1 Samuel 16:7-13: man's selection is God's rejection:

"But the Lord said to Samuel, "Do not look at his appearance or at his physical stature, because I have refused him. For the Lord does not see as man sees; for man looks at the outward appearance, but the Lord looks at the heart." So Jesse called Abinadab, and made him pass before Samuel. And he said, "Neither has the Lord chosen this one." Then Jesse made Shammah pass by. And he said, "Neither has the Lord chosen this one." Thus Jesse made seven of his sons pass before Samuel. And Samuel said to Jesse, "The Lord has not chosen these." And Samuel said to Jesse, "Are all the young men here?" Then he said, "There remains yet the youngest, and there he is, keeping the sheep." And Samuel said to Jesse, "Send and bring him. For we will not sit down till he comes here." So he sent and brought him in. Now he was ruddy, with bright eyes, and good-looking. And the Lord said, "Arise, anoint him; for this is the one!" Then Samuel took the horn of oil and anointed him in the midst of his brothers; and the Spirit of the Lord came upon David from that day forward. So Samuel arose and went to Ramah." (1 Samuels 16:7-13 - NKJV).

What looks favourable to man is not always favourable to God. Man will look at the outward appearance: your past and present, what they know, and hear of you and your personal appearance; man will focus on your mess, but God focuses on what He says about you. Many of us fall into the trap of rejection, and that helps spiral us down the wrong road, leading to us not realising we serve the God of the turnaround. You were rejected because God has selected you in this life for the King's table. This life was not by chance or without meaning.

Nothing you have been through will be wasted. Rejection was just a part of the ploy. It had to happen. However, know that it was powerful. If you were not rejected, you would have no idea what it feels like to stand on your own; in standing on your own, you realise your strength. If you were not rejected, you would never get the position where God could have you to Himself. If the world selected you, the world would have most of your time and energy. What selects you is what has most of your time and preference; what you put everything into until you become it.

Let me get your mind to where you realise that rejection was not only necessary but was a blessing. I could not be like my family, not like my friends, nor could I be what the world standards required. It was not who I was and who I was could not be contained by them. Therefore, rejection was the only thing they offered. People reject what they do not understand.

David's father could not select him because God had already made the selection concerning his life. My family, and even those in my past journey, could not select Stacy-Ann Garvey because God had already selected and called me Resurrected Garvey. What was meant as a stumbling block was a channel for divine elevation. It is where you come to a place of understanding that you are not like others. The rejection will catapult you to a place where you realise that your life is to empower and is controlled only by God. Look at this fact: out of all his brothers, David was the only king. Out of all his brothers, David made history. Out of all his brothers, David was remembered. Out of all his brothers, David left a legacy that impacts lives even today. A very famous Scripture from David is "the Lord is my Shepherd." Can I tell you that there is power, life, and destiny in rejection? When you get to a place of understanding the true power and nature of rejection, you will be healed and made whole.

That day when the Holy Spirit opened my understanding to rejection, the journey of healing catapulted me to new levels. But it did not stop there for me; it was deeper because there was still a hidden prison that I had given no access to, not even myself. There was just too much vulnerability to reveal or even face. This prison was safely buried, and I had no reason to acknowledge it because I seemed to be doing okay, and I was delivered. I was lying to myself and going around in circles like a fool. This minute I would be fine, but then came the demons through the open door because I was lying to myself.

After I left prison and was home, I realised that relationships were one of my biggest struggles, not just romantic relationships but even regular friendships. I got into them for the wrong reasons, and they would not work. This would depress me and cause me to fight the spirit of oppression repeatedly. In my mind, I knew there were issues in my soul, and I did my best to deal with them through forgiveness and all but there was something still hanging.

I was home one night, and our country was going through a crisis, so social media was the go-to for communication services and ministry. My Coach, Crystal Daye, had a podcast called: "Diary of a Jesus Girl," and I decided to listen to it before going to bed. Her featured guest was Dr. Lorneka Josephs, speaking on the topic: "How to Powerfully and Practically Overcome Rejection." At first, I thought it was just one of those empowerment speeches where you hear how you can overcome and just move on: yada yada yada! The Holy Spirit messed up my thirty-eight years of existence; I am writing now and fighting the tears. I was undone; I was knocked off the horse of strength and became like a vulnerable little girl. The prison door of rejection just flew open, and I had to face it.

My father never showed me love as a child. I was never hugged and told "I love you" by him. I graduated to looking for it from my grandfather, but that did not work either. So, in my mind, that was normal. I was never like all my family growing up; I behaved differently. I spoke my mind, and I was always a leader. I was never timid, just mouthy. I realised that my cousin that I grew up with was loved by my family. They always treated her better than me, and even when we got stuff from abroad, they would give her the nicer stuff in my eyes. I saw them show her love, so in my eyes, something was wrong with me. My eyes were different, my skin, and even my weight. I developed an attitude that said "do as your cousin" so they could love you too, but that did not work. I developed a mindset at that age to do what other people were doing or try and be someone so they would love and accept me.

I became bitter after my first relationship failed, after doing everything for him to love me and realising that it did not work. The loss devasted me and left me hating loss and failure. Why had life been so mean to me is something I could not figure out or wanted to deal with. This spirit of rejection had followed me my entire life, and I did not know that the wound had traveled from childhood, attracting demonic spirits and sickness that would try to destroy my life. Because of this, I had not been able to have a healthy and prosperous relationship with any man.

My father had treated my smaller sister like his only daughter and left me, his eldest, to search for love. I did not know the love of a man or what it should be, so the first chance I got to experience it, I just went for it. I did so many experiments with my male and female acquaintances while growing up with my grandparents. My grandmother kept tenants whose single parents worked miles away in Kingston. I remember us playing dolly house, and I would allow so many explorations with my body, even though I did not understand what I was doing. I remember a female cousin that would visit my grandmother for summer holidays teaching me oral sex. I did not know it was oral sex but did it because I wanted to feel accepted by that cousin.

As much as I was now saved and given a new name, the prison of rejection was still very much up and running. Rejection had made me afraid to love and even receive love. Rejection made me always want to gain people's acceptance. I would always try to fit in, even if that was not for me. Rejection made me a very insecure woman, so I was always afraid of being judged because I looked different or dressed a certain way. Rejection caused opinions to affect me, whether good or bad. I would pretend in public, but when I was alone, I would lock away and cry. Rejection caused me to always want to change who God called me to be. I just wanted to make sure I was always accepted. Rejection has been the wall that has blocked me from total deliverance and mind renewal in terms of relationships. I was afraid to love and lose or being cheated on, which, in my mind, suggests that I was not enough. I held this prison so tight, and I did not want to let it go. I was oh so bitter!

It was time to let it go, and I had to start by first being open with myself with tears and the pain that came with the memories. One of the biggest reasons I desired a relationship, and even sex, was because I did not enjoy being alone. As much as I was in prison for years, I never mastered the art of being by myself. I always had to have a friend to keep me company or just someone in my corner. Of course, we need people and, no, we cannot live this life all alone, but I had never learned the art of enjoying my own company. I had never taken me out on a date or gotten to know me.

Marriage is my portion, but who am I, and what would I be offering to that man of God? Not dealing with issues such as this has been the source of destruction for many marriages. I am not an expert, but this is a clear indication that you being whole and healthy is very important because this is what you are joining to someone else. I always wondered why I felt disconnected from any sex partner I had and never had a memorable experience.

I decided to pack it up and give it all to God; everything that came with the rejection: insecurity, jealousy, doubt; everything. I cried for a few days, had a conversation with myself, and then I let it go. I also decided to trust God with my life totally and never take it up ever again. I let it go.

My decision to let it go led me to research the spirit of rejection and the benefits that come from being rejected. This brought me to some powerful teachings from Apostle Joshua Selman. I learned that there are signs and signatures that will show you a true man or woman that dwells in the secret place. I learned that anointing, power, and ministry do not show your divine connection with God, but the first sign of such is genuine brokenness. These are persons who have experienced pain and circumstances to a level where only God can fix them, so they have learned to dwell in His presence because they understand that their lives would be nothing and of no value without it. I began to marvel at the fact that you can tell when someone has had an encounter with God by the damage in their flesh. This, for me, was rejection.

Psalms 51:17, *"The sacrifices of God are a broken spirit: a broken and a contrite heart, O God, thou wilt not despise."*

The strength of God never comes to strong people who have it all together; it comes to weak and messed up people. My rejection was my sign of brokenness, and it was what humbled me and made me a candidate for the secret place in God. I had an opening that God could pour into. A broken man is one satan cannot dwell inside of because he is always before God. I learned, from the Scripture, that it is difficult for God to ignore a broken man. With this understanding, I prayed this prayer after hearing the teaching:

> *"Lord, here I am, Your child, Stacy-Ann Garvey; I am nothing before You: broken, full of mistakes, a mess who keeps on missing the benefits of rejection. Lord, let Your mercy and grace speak for me. I do not trust myself to fully capitalize on what You have allowed me to go through. I don't know what my emotions and vulnerabilities are; I have not gone far enough into purpose and destiny to know what I can do, so, Holy Spirit, teach and guide me. Father, I thank You for the rejection that allowed me to experience brokenness that has given me a key to remain in Your secret place.*
>
> *You declared that marriage is my portion; today, Lord, send help concerning marriage and let my mind not wonder on any residue from the past that came as a result of rejection. Align my heart and mind to healthy relationships as I am now walking into a healthy place. Deliver me from the scars and broken places of the past. Deliver me from jealousy that causes my mind not to think properly.*
>
> *Father, I pray for my husband that You, Lord God, will begin to bring a change into his life wherever he is, and You will align us together today, in the name of Jesus. Father, begin to transform his mind and life to that of a husband. Lord, break any illegal soul ties that he has attached to his life. Father, breathe Your mercy*

that has no condition or requirements upon him today, in the name of Jesus.

Today, let relationships in my life have meaning and reflect answered prayers. Father, today, show Yourself mighty in this area of my life where yesterday I suffered so many defeats. Today, Lord, I need a change. Show Yourself mighty today in my relationships."

Anger

I was about five or six years old when I woke up one night and saw my parents playing—I thought they were playing. I sat up staring as the lights were on. I saw the "playing" get intense until I heard my mom crying out for help and saw a helpless look on her. Something inside me caused me to jump up, grab a mop, and start hitting my father with it. My dad just lifted me like a ball and threw me on the bed, not to harm me but to get me to stop. I remember telling him, "Leave my mommy alone."

They were fighting again another day after we had moved to another house. I ran inside the kitchen and took a pot this time and hit him; I was about seven years old. I hit him with so much force as anger had now taken root inside my heart.

My parents broke up and re-kindled about four to five times while I was a child until they ultimately separated. I really loved my mom. As a child, she was the prettiest girl in the world; always dressing up, wearing makeup and nails, plus different hairstyles. My mom is a beautiful woman, but life had messed with her the wrong way. From what I gathered, my mom had me in her teens, so educational opportunities she wanted never became a reality as my brother came three years after me. Her dreams of becoming a nurse was now a long-gone reality. She never had the greatest relationship with her mother as well as her family. My mom was feisty and different; I know where I got it from!

I remember seeing her go through abusive relationships, but she fought. So many people did her wrong. I think I remember just once in her life where she looked comfortable, but it was short-lived as the man who helped her achieve that little comfort level was killed right before my eyes at a party my mom was hosting at her bar; I was thirteen years old.

With all I saw my mom go through, I became very angry, and that anger that followed me into adulthood. I had the mentality that no man could ever hit me, or a morgue would pick him up. I decided from a child that I would be independent because no man would ever take me for a fool. I was so angry at the world without realizing just how angry I was until a situation came up.

I remember in my relationship with my first son's father, I fought with this man, who was way bigger than I was, and I did not care. Praise God, he was never physically abusive to me, or God would have had to step in on my behalf. I destroyed things whenever I got angry. I remember getting so angry to the point of no control. I was so angry at how men treated my mom that it pushed me to always be independent. That independent nature was so strong that my constant thought was, "I must get this on my own no matter what." That mentality cost me my freedom.

In prison, I was angry with friends who had turned their backs, and I kept telling myself that I would get revenge because they had all hurt me. People I thought would be there just left, and they did not just leave, they stabbed me in the back. I was all alone and angry.

My Prison Break

In evaluating my life and the anger, I realised that I was not just angry at my dad, exes, or friends who let me down, but I was angry with myself more than anything or anyone.

Anger had overtaken my life; it took charge, and it felt like I could not do anything about it. I was angry with me. I felt like a disappointment all my life, and it seemed that when I loved something, I would lose it, and I was unable to make the dreams I had become a reality. I felt like a failure because of the many mistakes I made and because of all that I had bottled up. I was so angry that it caused me to sink deeper into depression.

I always enjoyed writing, so what the Holy Spirit began to do with me was allow me to start writing a daily journal and prayers to God. This allowed me to empty my heart to the Lord daily. I would write how I felt; I was turning over a new leaf, and I also began to write the vision and the new goals I had for my life. I wrote letters to people I knew would never read them, but it healed me from the anger because I let it out. Gradually, the walls disappeared, and my healing began. Truthfully, the process began while incarcerated, but it took time to release all the residue.

CHAPTER 11
UNCOVERING THE SCARS

While in prison, the Holy Spirit took me on a journey to studying the Word. I was going through Scriptures while healing and growing. The greatest victory we can ever have over the enemy is to expose ourselves before he does. I remember listening to Prophetess Sarah Smith, who was so bold when she spoke of her past, leaving no stone unturned. She had no qualms in saying how it was. The true power of a man is to be truthful when a lie is required. For most of my life, I lived a lie. My appearance was a lie; my life from the outside would be a lie, causing my speech to also become a lie. Life has taught many of us to bury our truth because our truth does not fit the world's standard, or it does not fit the requirement to be known or noted as someone of value in this world. No matter how dirty, messy, nasty your truth is, it always has value. It is your truth, and no one can emulate or try to be your truth. Your truth was not designed to stay hidden; the truth carries a light that, no matter the colour it is painted, will enlighten because it is the truth.

The journey to write this book allowed me to come face to face with many things. The most profound for me was uncovering scars and looking deep in the womb at the truth. It was never easy admitting to anyone that I had committed abortions. It was never easy telling anyone I had committed fraud and went to prison. It was never easy telling people that for all my life, I really did not have a man for myself or one who could really, truly love me. It was never easy admitting that I bought love or paid friends to do things for me or even that I visited an obeah man to buy love at a point in my life. It was never easy admitting my mistakes, coming face to face with the fact that I felt as if my family really did not love me. How could they perform an action if they had no idea how to love?

The biggest obstacle many of us face daily is admitting who we really are. Romans 8:1, *"There is therefore now no condemnation to them who are in Christ Jesus who walk not after the flesh but after the spirit."* This is a fundamental truth that resounded with me and will never leave. I understood the Scripture; I fell in love with it; there is nothing I have ever done or will ever do for the Lord to condemn me. Once Christ does not condemn me, I am at liberty to walk this journey in total freedom from any baggage that comes from the truth of who I was. So, I began to be truthful to myself.

The first question I asked was, "Who am I?" When I asked that question, I could not answer. I believed a lie for so many years that I was a depressed, low down, no good, messy, dead thing who was just existing. That day when I asked that question, and I could not answer, I prayed. I asked the Holy Spirit to take me on a journey to discover who I am. I did not just want to be someone who existed, but who was I really? What was it about me that He chose me? I wanted to be reintroduced to Stacy-Ann Garvey. Once I started reading and understanding the Scripture, I went on a journey where I lived and believed a life that surpassed all I ever went through. I did not feel as if I was worthy, but God was determined to change that.

When I was growing up, I always loved singing. I was so in love with music. The Lord gave me a voice. I loved reading books and writing. When I felt rejected by my family, writing was a way of expressing my thoughts. I loved reading as it took my mind to places where I wanted to go. I read lots of romance books and dreamt of Prince Charming rescuing me from a life I felt was boring. Life has a way of causing you to forget those things when the pressure of life messes with you. I remember when I was sixteen years old, I had my first encounter with the Holy Spirit at a youth retreat in Font Hill, St. Thomas.

That experience ignited something inside of me and started a fire. Even though life had tried to drown my fire, it was still burning somewhere on the inside. At that time, that experience gave me a divine connection, and my first encounter with my Father and caused my heart to experience a love that could only come from God. I used to visit my grandmother's room and sat in front of her wardrobe on a mat, with her Bible, and communicate with God. I would sing, listen, and communicate with Him; hours upon hours of basking in His presence At that time, God was planting seeds within me, but for some reason I did not know it. Those seeds planted remained; my heart, as much as it had experienced turmoil, still remembered those seeds planted. Today, I still desire those encounters with the presence of God

While serving time in prison, after reading some Scriptures, I heard the Lord say, "Build relationships through My Word." One morning I awoke and heard the Lord say, "Do time with Me again." I awoke wondering what that meant. I was reading my Bible, so I thought I was doing time with Him. While getting ready, some persons came and asked if I wanted to join the prison choir. Without hesitation, I said "Yes." What the choir did for me was reignite a fire I had for music; I loved singing, but I stopped. While on the choir, I was told that every November there was a crusade in the prison. I was excited; the crusade's theme was: "Doing Time With God." I just laughed. When I first heard it, I did not understand what God was saying. Preparation for the crusade bought me into a revelation that my prison sentence was not a sentence but time with God. The Lord was preparing me for restoration, and the only way He could do that was in prison.

My Prison Break

The call and anointing on everyone's life is different, and the anointing is at a cost. My restoration had to be done in isolation because of how deep I was in the mess that was my life. The truth is, I was a liar, thief, drug addict, alcoholic, abortionist, adulterer, and a total mess. I was the woman at the well; taking different men who did not belong to me. For God to purge and make me whole, it required me to do time. For me to also be analysed, I had to do time; the truth is, we conform to what we are around. I conformed to all of these things, so God had to teach me to conform to Him, so I could be identified with Him in spirit and truth.

Being in prison and spending time with God began to teach me who I was: a Royal Priesthood.

"But ye are a chosen generation, a royal priesthood a holy nation, a peculiar people; that ye should shew forth the praise of him who hath called you out of darkness into his marvellous light." (1 Peter 2:9).

I believed the truth of God and I started to live according to this truth from behind the walls of prison. The Holy Spirit educated me on how to live and operate as a free person; to be in respect and obedience to those placed over me. I learned to serve, which taught me the value of servanthood. One of the best medicines I received in prison was the gift of happiness and waking every day with a smile because I had life. I became highly active in prison; I participated in and organized programs for rehabilitation. I had established excellent relationships with officers and inmates as God was leading and teaching me fellowship.

It is never an encouragement for anyone to be in prison, but my prison experience was necessary for me to become who I am and for me to find the real me. I found joy in singing, reading my Bible, and praying; something I had not experienced in years, and it felt so good. I learned how to survive in a tight place when it required death. When I looked in the mirror and asked myself, "Who am I?" I smiled and had an answer. I was in a physical prison now filled with joy, peace, and love. I had been freed from the mental prison of the enemy. I experienced my prison break from behind the walls of Fort Augusta Adult Correctional Centre.

The beautiful thing about God is, He chooses people who are unlike the roles He has given them. You will find that He will choose unlikely individuals to carry His mantle. He chose a Rahab to save a nation; Jeremiah who said he could not talk; Moses to lead a nation and Gideon's army, which had no experience to win battles. What God does is select people who, in human terms, do not fit the status quo. God does all this to allow us to understand that it is He who makes the difference. Hence, we can boldly say He does not call the qualified, but He qualifies the called. When the Spirit of God enters your life, you become all that God calls you to be.

God has embarked on a mission to raise people that do not fit society's standards but fit kingdom standards. These people have survivors' stories and will make an impact on all those they come across. These empowered people will carry out the mandate of establishing the kingdom of heaven here on earth, as they realise that their lives are not their own but God's. God will save them from their dormant existence, resulting in them living a life serving God: evangelising about the kingdom of God and leading others to the kingdom. Your story is not one to be hidden, so take the limitations off. You do not know how powerful your pain will be to someone else. Your survival story can cause a chain reaction, resulting in many other's survival. Do not allow the devil to end, shut down, or stop your story because of the shame and disgrace of the past things you have done or who you think you are. Understand the truth of God; He makes the difference, and He can use anything and anyone.

PART IV
YOUR PAIN IS WEALTH

CHAPTER 12
PAIN WAS NECESSARY

After I was released from prison, I had to start over, and this was how God would process me because the promise of the Abrahamic blessings was on my life. The Scripture says that after suffering for a while, God will make you perfect.

"But the God of all grace, who hath called us unto his eternal glory by Christ Jesus, after that ye have suffered a while, make you perfect, stablish, strengthen, settle you." (1 Peter 5:10).

In my mind, I thought the suffering the Scriptures spoke of was my life in prison. I had this notion that God would establish me upon my release. This was not the case. I had plans to go home, get married, have another child, get a house, and operate a business; all would be well. I had already suffered, and God would see me through. All I needed to do was go to church every Sunday, sing praises, and all would be well with my soul; I was in for a rude awakening.

I realised that our plans are nothing compared to the plans of God. I realised that once you give God your life, He must be in control by any means necessary. He will disrupt your life to push you to the level He ordained before you were born. Going home made me realise what it meant to be anointed. When I was in the prison and on the choir, I thought that was ministry, the ultimate ministry for my life. I got a wakeup call; there was more to me than I even knew.

I started a relationship when I came home with a young man I met behind bars. I began to center and make my plans around this young man. While I was planning, the enemy was also planning, but God had the bigger plan. That relationship did not last more than two weeks as the requirements was not approved by God. When that happened, depression started knocking at my door. In my mind, I had failed another relationship. As much as I was college-educated in prison, I was not given practical experiences on how to conquer my depression. Here is the journey.

When depression started knocking again, I started visiting my father's establishment every Friday night: a bar. In my mind, one drink was not sinning against God. God understood that I was again fighting my depression. I still had residue that needed cleansing. I started working at a company, and I met someone who was more than a best friend, a confidante, someone who exhibited love and care, and a really good friendship. This soon blossomed into a relationship, one I was ashamed of; this person was married. I knew and felt like a dog returning to my vomit, and it was like my heart had no control. I was ashamed of myself. When I wanted to end the relationship, turmoil came. My mother, who was my number one support while incarcerated, started to have issues with me. Parents can be very controlling, and we were not seeing eye to eye, so she asked me to move out. With the assurance that this young man would help as he would stay with me while I was living with my mom, I moved out and into a house where the rent was JA$30,000, while I had an income of JA$35,000.

I remember soon after moving out, the pastor at the church I was attending called me and said, "The Lord said no to the relationship I was in." I did not tell her I was in a relationship in the first place. It was plaguing my mind, but I ignored it. I attributed it to her not seeing me at church as often; she was only saying that. A month later, I was asleep when the Holy Spirit woke me at 4 AM and gave me a glimpse of my future. What I saw in that vision caused me to wake with a different mind-set. The mind-set was so powerful that I ended the relationship with this man. I asked no questions about how I would survive. When I moved from my mother, the plan was for him to be my help. All I heard in my ear and the song on my heart was, "Surrender your heart to God." That is the reason why He saved me.

I started the journey in total repentance to God, being reminded that He had set me free, and that is how I must be: free. I went to God, fasted, prayed, repented, recommitted my life, and gave God my all. In 2015, I received a word that God was going to take me through a season known as the Refiner's Fire. I had no idea what that meant, but, oh my, was I in for a treat. I had done Bible study in prison with the Chaplin assigned, but I required more. I was going to church, serving my leaders, but something inside me kept crying for more. I knew there was more, and I wanted more. I began to search for it. I prayed and sought the Lord. I had a best friend, someone the Lord allowed in my life, to save me when the residue of suicide came knocking. She was my best friend and someone who holds a special place in my heart even today. She introduced me to my very first mentor and my spiritual father, Reverend Dr. Leostone Morrison. That was when I stopped drinking milk and started eating hard food.

There were lessons I learned while incarcerated, but there was more. There was more to pain, and the Lord was ready to take me to that place, teaching me that my pain was necessary. I read the Bible, but I never went in-depth. With God, nothing is as it seems. I started the prison journey, but God had to refine me to get me to that place. The Lord began to teach me that as a believer, I had to endure pain so I could be made perfect according to the will of God, lacking nothing. He requires perfection, and in order for me to achieve perfection, pain is required to teach me patience, perseverance, and long-suffering, which God said is a gift. In that season, God showed me that my pain was necessary to get me where He required me to be.

CHAPTER 13
ENDURING THE PAIN

Job 1:21 speaks of coming naked from my mother's womb and returning naked. The Lord gave, and the Lord taketh away, blessed be the name of the Lord. Let us pause for a minute and say, "Hallelujah!" To someone reading this now, if you are going through something, anything, pain; begin to shout like you are crazy; shout some Holy Ghost-filled praise because there is still a God in heaven who looks high and low, and you are in for a win. Praise, not because He has already done it, but because you are expecting Him to shift it for you.

Job was in a state of pain: having lost it all and being stripped of everything, yet he praised God. He praised God when he had nothing. I learned from Bishop T.D. Jakes that your nakedness can mean you are exposed. With all being exposed on Job, he did not crumble and buckle under the pressure; he praised. How many of us as believers can God allow to be exposed, and we still praise Him? The Lord said to satan, "Have you considered my servant, Job?" The Lord knew His servant, and He also knew the devil. Get ready; God already knew what He placed in Job. He knew Job would be victorious, and He knew that restoration would have been Job's portion. As a matter of fact, He knew Job's latter would be far greater than his former. He allowed the enemy to stir up the shift for Job. God will allow the enemy to bring forth disturbance in your life to get you to your latter. He is God.

The enemy is cunning, and he knows we are most vulnerable in our pain and suffering. His aim is to keep us from getting where God is taking us by keeping us focused on the situation and not the promise. We make the mistake of doing what the pain requires of us, going into depression, losing hope, and losing faith and dwelling there in our situations. Dr. Junita Bynum said it best. She said, "Some people keep saying, 'Why me?' but 'Why not you?'" You see, believers, you need to understand that you were chosen by the highest God to endure hardship as a good soldier so you will be qualified (See 2 Timothy 2:3-5).

When God allows you to go through a trial, He already knows the outcome. You are going to win because He is your Father: the victorious God. God said He will never give you more than you can bear (See 1 Corinthians 10:13). Whatever your pain is: bills, relationship, job, court case, anything; tell it that God has already given you dominion over them, and they are just an instrument to ignite your praise. Remind your pain that it is an opportunity for God to be exalted, and it is just for a period. God trusted Job with trials, and He will also trust you with it.

These lessons for me were practical teachings; I had to learn that God cannot lie, and if He calls you a survivor, you have to survive something. There are some lessons God cannot teach you in theory. I came to these realisations when God taught me that I was no longer drinking milk but was now ready for hard food. The day I accepted and said yes to where He was taking me was the day I opened the door to affliction.

I remember when I came home, my mother kept pointing out the bills and things to be done. I realised I had to do something as the pressures of life had begun to take a toll. I started selling bleach and soap on the roadside in Linstead, St. Catherine. I knew nothing of selling, but I knew I had a child depending on me and a mother continuously reminding me of the bills to be paid.

One day, I was returning home with the heavy containers of bleach, and I started having back pains. I remember saying to God, "This is not my portion." That day, Police Officers were trying to get the vendors off the roadside, and I did not know what to do. When the Police saw me, they shook their heads and walked by. That night when I got home, I cried, and I said, "Lord, I need You." The following day, on my way to Linstead to sell, I received a call for a job. I kept that job from 2014 to 2018.

Even though I had a job, things were never easy. I had to trust God for everything in my life. Trusting God was never easy. I grew up being an independent person who only knew how to depend on myself for what was needed. That is what I was used to. Finding Christ was my new life, and God saying to me, "I will do it for you." I had no idea how to do it, and it was hard to give up my will for the will of Christ. That is the story for many of us today: we have never had anyone who cared or loved us in such a way that everything that concerned us mattered to them. Realising that we are no longer alone is extremely hard for us. It is a difficult journey; the truth is, we do not know how to give up our will for the will of Christ.

I love how the Scripture shows us how God spoke on Job's behalf. It shows him to be tried by the enemy, and that is the story for many of us. God entrusted Job with trials, and so the story goes for many of us when God trusts us with trials. We get blinded by what we are going through that we fail to see the bigger picture. We get so lost in what we are going through that we fail to see that there is a reason why God is allowing us to experience our trials. Even though I received deliverance in prison, the residue was still affecting me. The failed relationship and depression had me turning to alcohol. This is the pattern that is affecting many today; the pattern of falling into what we were used to. We return to those patterns which did not work in the first place, instead of going to the source. God had to allow situations to occur for us to be overcomers. He must allow us to face our demons for us to be truly known as conquerors. You cannot conquer what you have not faced. God knew Job could do it, and He knows you can too. Remember, God had a relationship with Job, so He knew He had equipped Job with the tools to face his trials.

The Lord equipped me with the situation of being in prison for the trials to come. I will not sit here and say it was easy; it was not. What I will say is: what was planted in me—the power and grace of God—gave me the tenacity to sit in the refiner's fire to clear the residue that was in me.

Today, I encourage you to know that the obstacles and tests being experienced were never to kill you but to prove who God called you to be. God has confidence that you will come out as pure gold, so He has allowed you to be placed in the fire. Your value will be known after you have been placed in the fire. Diamonds are precious stones, and it is through testing in the refiner's fire that their true worth is revealed. Without the refiner's fire, diamonds are simply stones. Similarly, your trials and obstacles are the fires needed for your true self to come forth.

You were created in the image and likeness of God. After going through your process, your value will not only be known while you are alive but will leave a legacy after you have gone to be with the Father. You will never lose your value; your only job is to endure the pain.

CHAPTER 14
INTEGRITY IN PAIN

A particularly important component to integrity is pain when obedient: trusting God when He says no and not doing it our way because it seems easier. We need to ask God's permission before making any decision, even when the flesh needs it. The flesh must be subjected to the Spirit (Romans 8:7). In all your experience, have an attitude of gratitude; maintain your joy, and fuel your fire with joy. Fight with your praise. Go through as Christ: humble but keeping your eyes on Jesus.

Deciding in my mind and heart that I was now in a place where my value in God was more important to me than what the world had to offer, I decided to endure in my season. I remember the first house I lived in: I was thrown out and taken to court as I was unable to pay the rent. This was one of the most embarrassing, hurtful, and harsh experiences I have had since returning to society. There were so many people who did not believe I was going to make it due to my past and who I was. There are so many people who desire my hurt and for me to fail because, in their eyes, all I was known for was my past mistakes, and they could not see beyond that.

When I was thrown out, I was given a place to stay. I was assisted by a church sister. I prayed, dirtied my knees, and said, "Lord, I am ready to start over." I also believed I had failed. I also believed it was due to the sin I committed once I returned from prison. This caused me to repent for something God had already forgiven me for, but I did not know. I had already experienced seasons where I had to pray morning, noon, and night just to have food to eat. The truth is, it was hard, it was rough, and there were times I wanted to give up and throw in the towel, but there is always that small still voice that kept giving me the courage to keep going.

After I moved in 2016 and started over in my mind, I went to a crusade at a church in Berwick, St. Catherine. This church was pastored by a special spiritual father who God allowed to carry me for a season while going through the wilderness. When I went to the church, there was a pastor ministering: Bishop Musa Laing. While there, he called me and said, "The Lord will take you through a season, but the season will feel as if you are going to die, but the season is not to kill you but to build you into who He wants you to be." Apart from feeling super afraid and nervous, I kept thinking, "What more can I really endure?" I went home, cried, and started trying to convince God that I could not do it; it was already too much. Somehow, I could not find the courage to ask God, "Why me?" I already knew His answer would be, "Why not you?"

The week after that, every utility got disconnected at the same time. I maintained my peace as I received the word, and I said, "Okay, God, I will endure." Much to my surprise, it was much more than that. Things got so bad. I was dropping my son off at a Day Care where I had a huge bill; I could not make the payments. I would literally pray, reminding God that He gave me the job, so if He does not provide the favour for me to get to work, I would not be able to go. At that time, I was not receiving a salary because it all went to loan payments. I needed the job; it was still a source of survival. There were times while at work that I was unable to find food to eat, but the Lord would allow a young lady to give me half of her lunch every day. I saved it and took it home for my son to take to Day Care the following day.

I would be on fasting most days at work; that was the only way my mind would soothe the hunger I was really feeling. It was so bad that there were times I felt like I was losing my mind. The hunger was real. There was a time when every Saturday I would stay by my phone praying for someone to message me so I could ask them to help with food for my son. I remember when my son's father lost his job for a short period of time; things became so rough. I cried. I did not feel like I could continue because I did not see a way out.

I was coming from work one day with some dog food I had collected from co-workers; I always collected food scraps for my puppies. I remember having the lunch I was taking home for my son that I could not touch; it had to serve him for the following day. I remember while on the bus, I was so hungry because I did not eat for the entire day, and I hardly ate the days before. The hunger caused my body to start shaking; I felt like I was going to blackout. My mouth started getting dry, and I could literally feel my lips getting white. I had no money to buy anything; all I had was my taxi fare to go home to Ensom City. Ensom City was too far from Spanish Town for me to walk home, and the weakness I was feeling would not have allowed me to get home. I had to decide on the options I had. I ate the dog food to save my life at that moment. The food was inside a box, so no one noticed that it was dog food. It did not look horrible; someone had eaten and left a few chewed bones and what they did not want. That day, I closed my eyes but saved my life so I could be here today telling my story.

Loan companies were calling, sometimes visiting my workplace. I had fallen into the trap of living from loan to loan. At first, I was taking loans to pay bills and buy food as the salary, and the support from my son's father was not enough to pay bills, buy food, support my son and take us through the month. Living on loans became my reality. It is easy for many to judge but unless someone has been in the position, they will never understand. It got so bad that the loan companies kept calling and driving me crazy. Even though I decided to endure and not go out of the will of the Lord, the enemy decided that there was a door for him to try and set up my destruction.

So, during this time, there were so many offers of an easier life; answers to my problem, way out; none of it was in the will of God. These offers came at a time when I needed help the most. Deciding to serve Christ in spirit and truth will cause you to lose friendships that you spend time building. Choosing to live for Christ will cause you to lose things and opportunities that you thought you needed to survive. Choosing to live for Christ will see life hurt you in such a way that it causes you to face things you had buried, and things you never expected to face. Choosing to live for Christ is a daily sacrifice that one must consciously make and endure, but it will be worth it.

So many offers came, so many solutions, and they all sounded good, looked good, and even felt good. I almost fell for it. Reverend Leostone Morrison wrote a book called "My Renewal," where he exposed Biblical secrets to a better you. It is easy for many of us to fall into the trap of the enemy if we are not clear and persuaded by the Word of God. We go through life seeing with our physical eyes and not our spiritual eyes. Many of us are stuck at the same level: same obstacles, and same warfare, because of where our minds are stuck. When we become children of God, He requires us to operate from the third dimension: operate from where He is. We do this by operating by His Word and what He says. All that I was experiencing for those years was a test and my practical exam. I failed those exams and tests for almost two years because my mind was not renewed. You can be delivered, but your mind is not renewed. If your mind is not renewed, you will return to the mess you were delivered from.

Before I went to prison, I believed in the fast lane, and getting involved in fraudulent activities was the way to live. I had my own solutions to what I was experiencing when I had no clue who I was and what I was experiencing. God allowed those afflictions to occur so He could get me to a place to minister and change me. God wanted to renew my mind. Reverend Leostone once said to me, "One of the things I love about you, my daughter, is that you are teachable." I remembered those words in 2018 after I had lost the job that I was so dependent on for survival. I asked God, "I am teachable? What is it that You are teaching me?" The Lord took me through a season where He began to renew my mind. I got a word from God, spoken over my life, declared over my life and some manifested. I was my own stumbling block because of where I was, and my mind had to be renewed.

I remember in 2017, I was sitting at my desk when Bailiffs were continuously calling. My mind was in turmoil, and I remember seeing a notification from Dr. Juanita Bynum where she was speaking of the multibillionaire's mind-set. At first, I tuned in as I heard the word "multibillionaire," and I needed money; my interest was sparked. Little did I know that that word was going to interrupt and shake up my way of thinking. In that Facebook live, she said God has this entire world in His hands, and she held a baseball and enclosed it in her hands. She spoke into my spirit, and I asked myself, "Stacy-Ann, why are you worried when God loves you and has you in the palm of His hand?" She also said that nothing the enemy does causes you to quiver or be shaken when you dwell in the third dimension with Christ.

It means that not even the bills should cause me to quiver. The Holy Spirit reminded me that day who I am and whose I am; that gave me power. I had the power to not hide from the Loan Collectors but to approach and speak with boldness. What I realised was that the enemy had attacked my finances in such a way, and God had allowed it because He wanted to deliver me. The Lord wanted me to have no residue when He births a ministry inside me to lead people to total freedom. God never wanted me to be a slave to money. When the loan collectors call and terrorise you, it forces you to lie, borrow, and steal. The Lord reminded me that I am not a money chaser; money must chase me. Even though I was experiencing an embarrassing financial situation, God was teaching me integrity. He showed me that I did not have to go out of His will: take a man or via illegal means. I had all the power in His Word, and I needed to activate His Word. The Lord taught me, in that season, that you can be true to God and maintain your integrity in pain, no matter the circumstances. We can stay true to God no matter what the circumstances require. It starts from the mind. When your mind is plugged into the Source, and you begin to operate according to the Source, your flesh will be under total subjection to the Word of God.

CHAPTER 15
PAINFUL WORSHIP

No one can hurt or cause you pain more than those who you love. The greatest commandment that Jesus gave is to love. This was a challenge I thought I had conquered until it came knocking.

"Then cometh Jesus with them unto a placed called Gethsemane, and saith unto the disciples, Sit ye here, while I go and pray yonder. And he took with him, Peter and the two sons of Zebedee and began to be sorrowful and very heavy. Then saith he unto them, My soul is exceeding sorrowful, even unto death: tarry ye here and watch with me. And he went a little further and fell on his face, and prayed, saying, O my Father, if it be possible, let this cup pass from me: nevertheless not as I will, but as thou will. And he cometh unto the disciples, and findeth them asleep, and saith unto Peter, What, could ye not watch with me one hour?" (Matthew 26:36-40).

It was a Good Friday evening, and the persons who I owed rent had left their church service and decided they were coming to collect what I owed. Also, there was a lady I owed money; she assisted me in 2016 with a loan she had consolidated. That evening when they came, apart from being angry, my eyes became open about the church and the deep issues that we have as a church.

Money has power over the church because it still has the ability to destroy and mend people in church. The Scriptures about love and being a brother's keeper are secondary when it comes to money. The fact is, we all have one Master, and heaven is one place.

The anointing and tongues are well exercised by Christians against other Christians when money is owed.

I confided in this church family because it was the first church I became a part of after leaving prison. They knew my struggles; they knew my pain and my inability to pay the rent for a season and the loan: all I had confided, plus all the assistance I received, was exposed. I was ashamed of the 36-year-old woman I was.

That night, sleep was uncomfortable; apart from my son kicking me off the bed, my mind was being kicked by the reality of my debt. Early that morning, I woke up wondering what was going to happen to me and what I should do. I was in so much debt, and it was all to survive in this life and be righteous. Going the wrong way for money was easy; the enemy was just waiting for me to say yes.

At the same time, I had struggled so much and tithed and planted so much seed in faith, just believing God for what He said about my life. Yet, I was seemingly sinking deeper, and the embarrassment for unpaid debt kept coming at me. I had faith, and I believed God, yet I saw nothing changing. I was still borrowing loans to pay loans. Everything in my life just surrounded loans, and I became tired. I prayed so many times until I began wondering if God was hearing me or if He was mad at me for the life I was living as well. I had no other help but God at this point: none.

While I closed my eyes to let the tears flow in worship, as I could not pray as I wanted to, Tasha Cobbs' song "Fill Me Up" was playing in my ears. I knew without the shadow of a doubt that all my wounds were necessary. I sat and thought of every wound that I had because of church hurt; from being asked if I had taken JA$5,000 from the offering plate, to being sent Scriptures about stealing from church, to being assisted with JA$30,000 to move when I was put out of my first home to help me find somewhere to live. When I was unable to pay it back, it turned into a horrible mess. I was unable to cover the rent again for where I was living, and that also turned messy. The embarrassment was heavy and came from an unusual place " church." I always thought that church did not hurt people. I was hurt and was now facing the ultimate betrayal, which was to love in a tight place when your heart is broken by those whom you pledge to love and serve.

I underwent the journey of starting to love and what real love is as I was determined to love. Because of this, the Holy Spirit had to uncover the real reason why love was a journey for me. After the tears flowed, I sat and did some deep thinking wondering why I was crying. It came to me that I was allowing situations and circumstances, what people said and did to me, to reflect on me and shape who I was. I realised the struggle was acceptance. It was me accepting who I was and who I am now. It got deeper than this. The Holy Spirit began to remind me of being a child, teenager, and early adulthood. I could see myself as if I sat before a mirror. Looking in that mirror, I realised I struggled with the identity of accepting myself for who I truly am: the copper colour skin and the brown eyes I hated because it made me different from my cousins and brothers. I hated the red hair that never seemed pretty enough, and the body I thought was imperfect as a teenager. I realised how hard I tried to fix myself; tried to fix everything that I thought was physically wrong. I did the makeup, clothes, shoes, hairstyles just so I could look pretty enough, so I could accept myself.

I thought my body was not good enough, and that was why my first relationship did not last; why my first son's father gave me so much trouble and why I could not have a successful relationship. I was so uncomfortable with myself. In that moment of reflection, the revelation that I really did not love myself was shown.

My Prison Break

I remember when the Lord took me through a season where He gave me specific instructions to not relax my hair, no makeup, no shaving of eyebrows; nothing was to be done. In my mind, God was taking me through a period where He wanted to teach me how to look like a Christian (lol). However, that was not it. I also remember, during that period, persons saw me and always commented that I was glowing. At the end of that period, the Lord said that He took me through that period to show me that it had nothing to do with my appearance but His glory that was now shining in my life. I missed what God was really saying to me. It was in this moment now, thinking about everything, that what God was really saying gave me a slap in the face. God was showing me just how much He loves me; He loves me so much that His glory keeps glowing on and through me. All God was saying is that He wanted me to love myself. Now that brought down another shower of rain; my face was flooded. I cried so much and looked in the mirror and told myself that I loved me.

I struggled to love because I did not love myself, and that was a huge barrier. I knew I loved God, and I had no control over my heart just loving God. My actions to serve Him despite all that was happening around me made me realise just how much I loved God. God wanted me to love myself so I could truly love others, leading to the ultimate proof that I loved Him.

Love repaired my heart, cleansed my mind, gave me the courage to forgive and move on. As a result, I was able to let go of all the church hurt; I was able to deal with the issues that harboured in my soul as a result of this. Love makes you powerful; gives you the attitude of a conqueror. I realised that I was truly free and unhindered by all that had happened. The anger towards the hurt was erased by love, and God could move in the situation and repair the breach. At the end of the day, it is all about the kingdom of God, and that is all that matters. Let me encourage you: repair the breach in your heart with love. Love is the most powerful weapon that you could ever use. Love will make you forgive and accept the apologies that you never received.

The Holy Spirit reminded me of Abraham's separation from Lot and how it seemed Lot had taken the best portion. The experience was painful for Abraham as Lot was his nephew and someone he loved.

Genesis 13:14-17: "And the Lord said unto Abram, after that Lot was separated from him, Lift up now thine eyes, and look from the place where thou art northward, and southward, and eastward, and westward: For all the land which thou seest, to thee will I give it, and to thy seed for ever. And I will make thy seed as the dust of the earth: so that if a man can number the dust of the earth, then shall thy seed also be numbered. Arise, walk through the land in the length of it and in the breadth of it; for I will give it unto thee."

There are times in our lives when we must, according to Bishop T.D. Jakes, learn the art of saying goodbye, not because of any love lost, hatred, or anything at all, but because destiny requires it. No matter how much we learn from persons in our lives, not everyone is meant to travel on your God-ordained journey; not everyone has the ability to understand the anointing on your life. Some want to control what God has placed inside of you or even tell you who you should be when that is not the Word of God over your life. Separation is not always pleasant, but it is necessary at times. Lot was a veil blocking Abraham's vision. Looking back into the Scripture, we realise where strife is mentioned between Lot and Abraham's herdsmen. Lot's journey with Abraham was for only a period; it was not forever.

I have had friendships I thought would last forever in my lifetime, and there were no warnings or indications that those friendships would come to an end. I remember having a best friend who, in my mind, we were joined at the hip. We even had our time of the month together. I valued that friendship to the point where I began losing my own identity because I was conforming to things I did not believe in to accommodate the friendship, when the anointing on my life required a greater sacrifice.

That is the thing: some people are meant to be in your life for a season, while some are meant for a lifetime. Your only job is to understand seasonal people versus lifetime partners. Lot was never a part of what God was doing in Abraham's life in regard to his future. His season had come to an end, even though they were related. Lot could not go where Abraham was destined. Abraham was the carrier of nations; he had no time for distractions, no time to be caught in fighting over a spot of land.

Many of us have been called to a global stage, and there are people who were specifically placed at different seasons in our lives to help us as our destiny helpers for that season, and then there are levels that they were never designed to handle. They cannot go where you are going, even those relationships that did not work out.

Lot was caught up with what his physical eyes could see, and that is where his mind-set was: on things that would pass away. How could a mind like that handle the blessings that God had in store for Abraham? Lot would have been a blockage to the word over Abraham's life.

The Holy Spirit reminded me that God said to Abraham: *"Lift up now thine eyes, and look from the place where thou art northward and southward, and eastward and westward. For all the land, which thou seest, to thee will I give it, and to thy seed for ever." (Genesis 13:14).*

The Lord then began to speak into my spirit saying, "Stacy-Ann Garvey, you are Mine. I love you, and I will never cause you no trial and error, and nothing will ever make Me turn my back on you; don't you know that you are strong? Haven't I commanded you to be strong?

Am I not the same God who kept you and took you out of prison? Your story is about pain. I allowed you to go through it so the wealth will come. The pain from the separation was necessary as the story was sure."

I remember one day the Lord said, "Reach out to every man that has ever hurt you. Cry if you must but forgive." It was never easy, but I did. I had a conversation with my first son's father, and it was amazing. Today I can say we are co-parenting well. The hardest reaching out was to my first boyfriend, but eventually, I did, and it was not a chummy conversation, but it went well; today, I freely say hello on Facebook.

I realised that my finances was the area I received the most attacks from the enemy; an area where I erred in many times from prison to coming home, making foolish choices. This was a plot of the enemy to destroy me yet again. My character was under serious attack as the enemy wanted to discredit me and my God-given integrity that God was building. My integrity did not come by might or power but from the Spirit of the living God, who is responsible for my new life. After hearing the Word of God regarding pain, I began to use pain to my advantage.

There were some changes I had to make personally, and I also had to work on myself and maintain integrity. Anything God starts, He completes. I had to develop confidence when it came to God in this area, which caused me to slowly fix areas that were out of control.

I remember losing the first job I had been so blessed with after prison. That job came and was kept by faith and just the favour of God. I had so many advantages on the job, and it afforded me many opportunities. I loved that job so much because it was the second chance I was given to reposition myself and make a difference. Losing it and the betrayal was one of the most painful experiences I had ever encountered since being home. What made it worse was that it cost me the best friend I had known since returning home to society. It took me a while to forgive and accept the reality, but I did through the Scriptures. That was land and cattle for a season; God had nations and continents waiting for what He had planted inside of me. I got comfortable on the job and was not focused too much on ministry anymore. I was caught up trying to make enough money to pay bills that I forgot God. I was distracted with the season and was losing sight of who God had chosen me to be.

When God ministered the word to me through the Scriptures, I was empowered. I was empowered to come to the knowledge that nothing in your life, as a child of God, will be wasted. Even the pain, hurt, and embarrassment will not matter. It is okay; many will profess that they are strong, and nothing is wrong with that. But unless you experience a situation requiring strength, you cannot profess to be strong.

I remember one day when the Lord called me "Resurrected Garvey." At first, I thought it was all in my mind. I changed my Facebook name from Flawless Garvey to Resurrected Garvey, not knowing the manifestation of what God was saying. I was too busy with life and what was happening to me to really sit and analyse what God was saying about me, until later when I saw something, and I researched what my name meant. What I found was that the name "Stacy" meant "Resurrection."

I was designed by God to counteract death and dead situations; that was a heritage I had, which was planted before I was placed in my mother's womb. When God whispered "Resurrected Garvey" in my ear, He was calling me by my name and who I really am. There were several times when God had to call me by my name for me to snap back into who I am and who I am truly called to be; the residue of not forgiving, rejection, and church hurt was conquered by the resurrecting blood that contains love, which God had placed inside of me. Love conquered; love won. Church hurt became null and void because love had the power to erase what the enemy was trying to do. Prophetess Sarah Smith said it best: "Do not harbour issues in your soul because the issues can send you to hell." It took the pain to lead me to total deliverance.

What God has placed inside you is to shift atmospheres, change nations, and affect regions and continents. You cannot afford to be caught in the web of the enemy because of land. The squabbles, unnecessary warfare, and bickering are not worth it; let it go. If Abraham had allowed the issue with Lot to keep him bound by affecting his heart, he would not have been free in his mind to see what God was showing him. God has been showing many of us our destinies, but because of our minds and the soul's condition, we have been blocking our vision. It is time to let go; break free because a spot of ground cannot compare to regions, nations, and continents.

Running this race called life is never easy, especially if you are full of scars, cuts, and bruises, which cause pain that sometimes slows you down and makes the finish line look far away. However, if you look at the situation through the lens of the Holy Spirit, I guarantee you would realise that in all things, you are more than a conqueror who will only get better and not bitter. You will run and not be weary, walk and not faint (See Isaiah 40:31).

The Holy Spirit downloaded a word in my spirit called "Overruled." This enforces the Word of God that says we are seated in heavenly places with Christ Jesus (See Ephesians 2:6). It means we are not under earthly jurisdiction, but the laws and principles of heaven govern us. The enemy does not have a say in our lives; he has no say in the outcome of our lives. He has no power over our destiny; we only need to learn how to push beyond the pain and keep running to the finish line. Bishop Noel Jones preached a word: "Sit On Me"; for us to keep running, we need the Holy Spirit to keep us in this race.

As children of God, we must understand that when we gave up all rights for our lives to God and were adopted into sonship, allowing our temples to be the dwelling place for the Holy Spirit, it means God is under divine obligation to take care of every aspect of our lives. God makes our lives His priority: teaching, providing, defending, covering, leading, and guiding us in every stage of our journey. God just requires a relationship with us that is daily sustained.

My pastor, Dean Smith, announced a theme at church called, "Pray Again." This was a turning point and a new level for me. This topic encouraged a next level of relationship with God, constantly communicating, in tune, listening, following, and just loving on Him. Being in love with Christ will make situations dim. We should be so focused on our relationship that nothing else matters. Crossing the finish line makes your legacy live on, even after you are gone. The wealth does not come from just crossing the finish line; the wealth comes from the pain.

My prison break came out of total submission to God, which caused me to come face to face with truth.

CONCLUSION

What God designed from the foundations of the earth for your life was for you to shift atmospheres, loose regions, and set continents free with the Gospel.

Irons and chains have no power over fire because fire melts and refines. Fire makes the difference. That is you! Yes, you were designed to make the difference. Every situation I went through was a process because God was refining me as He is refining you right now.

Today is your Prison Break!

What the enemy meant for evil, God always uses for your good. You see, being bound was necessary, but that is not how the story ends. Jesus had to allow death so He could follow protocol—which was His own standards—to go into hell and conquer it. If He did not allow death, then He would have breached His own principles.

"For the wages of sin is death; but the gift of God is eternal life through Jesus Christ our Lord." (Romans 6:23).

O death, where is thy sting? O grave where is thy victory? (1 Corinthians 15:55).

Death was the reward for sin. Jesus discredited the sin reward before He even said, in my words, "Look, I made Myself an example in the flesh and went through the protocol and have now given you power over sin." It is necessary; in order to conquer something, you have to experience it. What you experience, you will conquer today.

Let us get this thing right, family, the prison situation in your life was necessary so you would conquer. Prison represents the bondage many people are under today because they have not come to the knowledge that they are in bondage. Many people are walking around physically free but spiritually bound by things you were created to conquer: depression and demonic oppression, fear, alcoholism, lesbianism, abusive relationships, lies, anger, rejection, homosexuality, abortions, HIV, AIDS, and the biggest of them all, believe it or not, unforgiveness.

Today is your prison break; your mind will be renewed today. You will understand that you are not bound by it even though you had to go through it. You need to talk to your prison and begin to let go of what you are holding on to. It is time to tell the prison situation, "Thank you for the inheritance."

It was the prison situation that promoted you; that was all it was for. It was the prison that showed you what was inside of you. It was the prison situation that propelled you into destiny. Anything you survived, you have power over it, and that is also your ministry. If you have power over it, then you can show others how to also survive it. Purpose cannot die but, let me go further, purpose cannot stay bound. A person who has been broken and restored is a person the enemy can never stop again because brokenness gave them access to the King that shifted their entire existence.

Today, I am a brand-new woman; no longer Stacy-Ann Garvey but Resurrected Garvey: a testament of love and forgiveness. God has taken me from prison to promotion. What God has done in my life has taken me to levels that do not reflect the scars, but the benefits from the scars testify of His glory. I have learned that it was really not about me; nothing I went through was for me. God used me as a vessel to go through the mess to establish and save many.

I am a woman of wealth and power, a living testimony of how God can turn a mess into a miracle just because God chose an unusual vessel like me. God has chosen you; that is why you have been through so much. It is time now to arise and shine beyond what you have been through. You can do it!

I made the local news years ago for a crime I had committed. Today, I make the local and international news, blogs, status, and social media posts with a global impact for Jesus Christ because I allowed the pain to grant me wealth.

My prison was never Fort Augusta Adult Correctional Centre; it was my mind. My road to freedom began while I was incarcerated, and it took years to finally be free.

My Prison Break was not instant; it was a process that took years; a process that saw God causing old wounds to be opened for me to come face to face with the charges I had laid against my own life, and had sentenced my own destiny. God, however, stepped in and acquitted my life into everlasting freedom through Jesus Christ. I received a Prison Break to now become a Prison Breaker.

ABOUT THE AUTHOR

The Jamaican born Stacy-Ann Garvey is an author, motivational speaker, wealth and empowerment Christian coach, conference host, television personality, MC, visionary, and a minister of the Gospel. She gave her life to the Lord in 2010 behind the Fort Augusta Adult Correctional Centre walls, where she was serving a prison sentence. Hers is a story of a mess God turned into a miracle for His glory.

Stacy-Ann Garvey was chosen and qualified by God to tell others of Jesus Christ and to bring hope to those afflicted and cast aside by society. She is the visionary behind Resurrected Garvey Ministries and is currently a member of the Light of the Gentiles International Ministries, under the leadership of Pastor Dean Smith and Prophetess Sarah Smith. She serves as an usher, minister, and oversees the Singles Ministry.

She is the mother of two handsome sons: Kemar Goldson and Zane-Sanniah Johnson. She is a conqueror; whose story of survival is a testimony to many. Her life has been blessed, and as a recipient of God's favour, she uses her testimonies of overcoming great adversities and being rejected by family and society to empower and spread the Word of God to those greatest in need.

Stacy-Ann Garvey is a generation changer with the Word of God, bought and paid for by the Blood of Jesus. Her motto is: "Solo Scriptura – *Scripture Alone*."

www.ingramcontent.com/pod-product-compliance
Lightning Source LLC
Chambersburg PA
CBHW071218160426
43196CB00012B/2342